Financial Intelligence

How to Make Smart, Values-Based Decisions with Your Money and Your Life

by Doug Lennick, CFP®
with Kathleen Jordan, Ph.D.

The Financial Planning Association (FPA) is the membership association for the financial planning community. FPA is committed to providing information and resources to help financial planners and those who champion the financial planning process succeed. FPA believes that everyone needs objective advice to make smart financial decisions.

FPA Press is the publishing arm of FPA, providing current content and advanced thinking on technical and practice management topics.

Information in this book is accurate at the time of publication and consistent with the standards of good practice in the financial planning community. As research and practice advance, however, standards may change. For this reason, it is recommended that readers evaluate the applicability of any recommendation in light of particular situations and changing standards.

Disclaimer—This publication is designed to provide accurate and authoritative information in regard to the subject matter covered. It is sold with the understanding that the publisher is not engaged in rendering legal, accounting, or other professional service. If legal advice or other expert assistance is required, the services of a competent professional person should be sought. —*From a Declaration of Principles jointly adopted by a Committee of the American Bar Association and a Committee of Publishers and Associations.*

The views or opinions expressed by the author are the responsibility of the author alone and do not imply a view or opinion on the part of FPA, its members, employees, or agents. No representation or warranty is made concerning the accuracy of the material presented nor the application of the principles discussed by the author to any specific fact situation. The proper interpretation or application of the principles discussed in this FPA publication is a matter of considered judgment of the person using the FPA publication and FPA disclaims all liability therefore.

The Financial Planning Association is the owner of trademark, service mark, and collective membership mark rights in FPA®, FPA/Logo and FINANCIAL PLANNING ASSOCIATION®. The marks may not be used without written permission from the Financial Planning Association.

CFP®, CERTIFIED FINANCIAL PLANNER™, and federally registered CFP (with flame logo) are certification marks owned by Certified Financial Planner Board of Standards. These marks are awarded to individuals who successfully complete CFP Board's initial and ongoing certification requirements.

Financial Planning Association
4100 Mississippi Ave., Suite 400
Denver, Colorado 80246-3053

Phone: 800.322.4237
Fax: 303.759.0749
E-mail: FPApress@FPAnet.org

www.FPAnet.org

ISBN: 978-0-9798775-3-7
ISBN-10 0-9798775-3-9

Manufactured in the United States of America

About the Authors

Doug Lennick, CFP®, is CEO and co-founder of the Lennick Aberman Group. He is legendary for his innovative approaches to developing high performance in individuals and organizations and is an expert at developing practical applications of the art and science of human behavior, financial and otherwise.

Before founding the Lennick Aberman Group, Doug was executive vice president of advice and retail distribution for American Express Financial Advisors (now Ameriprise Financial). In that capacity, he led an organization of 17,000 field and corporate associates to unprecedented success. Although no longer full-time at Ameriprise, Doug retains the title of EVP and senior adviser to the chairman and CEO, Jim Cracchiolo.

Doug is co-author with Fred Kiel, Ph.D., of the internationally successful book, *Moral Intelligence: Enhancing Business Performance and Leadership Success* (2005 and re-released 2008, Wharton School Publishing), as well as author of *The Simple Genius (You)* and co-author with Roy Geer, Ph.D., of *How to Get What You Want and Remain True to Yourself.* Doug is in high demand as a keynote speaker as well as an executive and organizational adviser. He has been quoted and referenced in many publications and books, including Daniel Goleman's seminal book *Working with Emotional Intelligence* and Richard Leider's bestselling *Power of Purpose.*

In November 2000, Doug was honored by Columbia University's Center for Social and Emotional Education and is a Fellow at the Carlson Executive Development Center, Carlson School of Management, and University of Minnesota. Doug is a graduate of the University of Minnesota, Morris, and is currently a member of the prestigious Consortium for Research on Emotional Intelligence in Organizations.

Doug and his wife, Beth Ann, reside in Edina, Minnesota. Their younger daughter, Joan, is a recent graduate of Stonehill College in Easton, Massachusetts. Their older daughter, Mary, has a sociology degree from the University of Minnesota and is pursuing graduate studies at Augsburg College in Minneapolis. Doug's son, Alan, is a financial adviser with Schubert, Kumagai, Lennick & Associates, a financial advisory practice of Ameriprise Financial Services, and lives in Minneapolis with his actress wife, Sari, and their son, Dylan.

Kathleen Jordan, Ph.D.—Kathleen is a behavioral psychologist and writer. She was collaborating writer with Doug Lennick and his co-author Fred Kiel on *Moral Intelligence: Enhancing Business Performance and Leadership Success* (Wharton School Press, 2007.) She is also co-author, with Fred Mandell, of *Becoming a Life Change Artist: Seven Creative Skills That Can Transform Your Life* (Avery Penguin, 2010.) As a psychologist, Kathleen works with individuals and business leaders to enhance their personal and organizational performance. A long-time Boston resident, Kathleen currently lives in Colorado Springs, near her daughter Erin, a graduate student in accounting, son-in-law Doug, an Army officer, and granddaughter Mackenzie.

Dedication

To my wife, Beth Ann, who has been and continues to be the most influential role model in my life—and to my children Alan, Mary, and Joanie, my daughter-in-law, Sari, and my grandson, Dylan—and to my now deceased parents, Albert and Martha Lennick, and my sister, Carol. For all of them I have great love. They have made me a lucky man indeed and to them I will be eternally grateful.

About FPA

The Financial Planning Association® (FPA®) is the leadership and advocacy organization connecting those who need, support, and deliver professional financial planning. FPA demonstrates and supports a professional commitment to education and a client-centered financial planning process. Based in Denver, Colorado, FPA has 97 chapters throughout the country representing tens of thousands of members involved in all facets of providing financial planning services. Working in alliance with academic leaders, legislative and regulatory bodies, financial services firms, and consumer interest organizations, FPA is the community that fosters the value of financial planning and advances the financial planning profession. For more information about FPA, visit www.FPAnet.org or call 800.322.4237.

Table of Contents

Foreword

by Richard L. Peterson M.D

Have you ever bought at the top of a market bubble? Or sold into a market panic? Of course you have—we all have—it's part of being a human investor. For all the talk of rational investors, the past two years have shown us the awesome power of investor emotions in driving market prices.

Psychological tools for managing investor emotions have been developed only in the past decade. Doug Lennick is a pioneer in this work. He is one of the first to understand the practical, everyday challenges faced by investors attempting to think *rationally* while investing in obviously *irrational* markets.

As an executive who grew Ameriprise's Financial Advisory unit into one of the largest in the United States, and a co-founder of Lennick Aberman Group, Doug has been ahead of the crowd in recognizing the importance of two major cultural trends. Doug was among the first to see the broad public value of personal financial advisers. He was a visionary in seeing the emerging research on emotional intelligence as a harbinger of changes in our understanding of investors. Over his career, Doug designed and successfully deployed practical approaches aimed at solving these two major real-world needs: the need for individual financial advice and the need for help managing financial emotions and the mistakes they cause.

After I published *Inside the Investor's Brain,* Doug shared with me some of his thoughts and experiences from working with emotional investors. One of the most challenging aspects of our shared work in training investors and financial advisers was in helping investors manage unconscious (but destructive) financial emotions. After all, if such emotions are unconscious, then by definition one cannot see them. It's a Catch-22.

I asked Doug his thoughts on helping people avoid unconscious emotional mistakes. With characteristic optimism, Doug related the following analogy: "Suppose you've had a bad day at work—maybe you lost money in the markets, or a major client expressed doubts about your talent. After such a bad day, have you noticed that when you arrive home everyone seems inappropriately upbeat? On some level this aggravates you further. Somewhere in the back of your mind you might even think, 'Don't they know I had a bad day?' Maybe you slam a door, criticize someone, or start a petty argument—anything to bring them to your negative level. But usually the evening plays out with you sulking and them thinking, 'Oh, there he goes again, he must have had a bad day.' They get on with their cheerful lives, and you're left alone to bring yourself out of your own emotional funk."

Doug realized that we can't change our unconscious emotions and habits directly. We're often unaware of what we're feeling and how it affects us. However, by identifying and aligning our core values, aided by the use of analogies and story-telling to speak to the unconscious, the process of change becomes much smoother. Stories, provocative questions, and worksheets help the reader achieve greater financial intelligence (both consciously and unconsciously).

Financial Intelligence lays out a roadmap for successfully identifying values, managing unconscious emotions and biases, and living to one's highest potential. The wisdom of Doug's approach to defining and living by our guiding values becomes clear in this book. When we live in ignorance of our values, goals, and plans, we are more likely to meander into emotional traps and destructive habits with our money (and our lives!). By learning to use Doug's 4Rs technique, recognizing, reflecting, reframing, and responding, you'll gain a simple, powerful, and flexible tool for transforming your approach to difficult situations and overcoming ingrained habits.

Doug defines financial intelligence as "the ability to make smart, responsible, values-based decisions with and about money in the face of competing and difficult-to-deal-with emotions." With this book, Doug gives you the tools to raise your financial intelligence, but it's your responsibility to follow through on it. By thoughtfully reading and working through this book, you will reap lifetime financial and emotional benefits.

Remember to bring your pen, notepaper, and an open mind as you read. I wish you much wealth, health, and happiness in your life. I think you'll find *Financial Intelligence* an excellent guide on your financial (and life) journey.

Richard is author of Inside the Investor's Brain. *He is a managing partner of Market Psychology Consulting, has worked as associate editor at the* Journal of Behavioral Finance, *a psychiatrist, and a former trader. Richard also performed postgraduate neuroeconomics research at Stanford University.*

Introduction

t's easy to miss the turnoff for Laurie and Scott Keller's home in Still River, a historic village in the heart of Massachusetts orchard country. There, Laurie and Scott, a happily married couple in their late 40s, have created a haven for themselves and their large family of aging rescue animals. Both have demanding careers—Laurie is a freelance writer and editor and Scott is a technology entrepreneur. In 2004, a real estate boom was in full swing when they spotted an opportunity to invest in two pre-construction condominiums slated to be built in an old textile mill building in a nearby city. When Laurie and Scott saw the building, it was love at first sight. The model was beautiful. The river views were captivating. And Laurie felt a strong emotional connection to the building, since her grandparents had earned their living working in textile mills. Scott and Laurie both felt excited about helping give new life to this neglected historic building. They had no doubts about the wisdom of their investment. The location, close to a university and sports center, seemed ideal for future residents. Their only question was whether they should rent out the completed units or sell them outright for what they expected would be a sizable profit.

Then, on the evening of May 16, 2006, Laurie and Scott's perfect investment washed away in the storm waters that swelled the Merrimack River to its highest level in more than 70 years—forcing the evacuation of the just-restored mill building. They had been four days away from closing on one of the units when the river flooded. The buyer backed out. Eventually, they found another buyer to whom they sold the unit for a small loss. Laurie and Scott walked away from the other unit, forfeiting their deposit. Their financial loss wasn't catastrophic, but for them, it wasn't trivial either. It was money they would miss, money that could have gone into retirement savings. And they lost a bit of self-esteem. They knew they had made a mistake. They felt bad, thinking maybe they just weren't the kind of people who should invest in real estate. Today, reflecting on that episode in their financial lives, Laurie says that she and Scott learned a lot:

> We never had a contingency plan. We thought about how beautiful the river was, not about how it could flood. And we never researched the condo market in the area. If we had done our homework, we would have learned that there were hundreds of similar condo projects being built all over the area. What seemed unique to us—the history of the building and its connection to our family history—didn't matter, since we weren't planning to live there. When it was time to sell our units, we were competing with 250 comparable condominiums for sale.

WHAT'S TO BLAME?

Laurie and Scott's experience is not unusual. There are millions of intelligent, caring, and hardworking people who make financial mistakes every day—mistakes that may leave us saddled with debt, stuck with an unsellable investment property, or short on retirement funds. What's to blame for such mistakes? Our brains make fools of us. The emotional center of our brains tends to take over when we're faced with any significant financial situation. Whether we're captivated by excitement about "surefire" investments that will quadruple our return or depressed by the declining worth of our 401(k)s, emotions are at the heart of what can lead us to bad decisions about our money. Emotions are why we often buy more real estate than is appropriate for our portfolio. Emotions are why we sell good stocks worth half of what we paid for them, thereby locking in our losses. Emotions are why we buy things we can't afford, or buy things we can afford, but that keep us from investing in more worthwhile priorities. Emotions are also why we don't spend or invest money when we should. Out of fear, we may completely avoid stock investments that could help sustain us through our retirement years. Out of fear, we may not spend money on a vacation that could help our family bond. Even when we think we are being logical, we're often using logic to justify the emotional impulses that make a bad financial choice look so good.

There are other kinds of financial mistakes that are less obvious than those that visibly shrink our net worth. For instance, our decisions may be paying off for us in a strictly financial sense, but we're working so hard to make money that we don't have enough time for family, friends, or other things we really value.

HOW THIS BOOK WILL HELP

In this book, you'll discover why you have trouble making optimal financial decisions. You'll also learn how to make decisions that simultaneously grow your money, increase your sense of purpose, and enhance enjoyment of your life. In other words, you'll learn how to make money, keep more of the money you make, and most important, make your money matter. As the title suggests, financial intelligence is at the heart of your financial and personal well-being. Throughout the course of the book, you'll discover that there are a number of ways to bolster your financial intelligence.

First, you can make financial decisions that are aligned with your most important personal values. We increase the odds of having meaningful lives if we use our money in ways that support those values. If, for instance, we want our children to have good educations, but we don't save money for their education, we are making financial decisions that don't support one of our values. But if we decide to spend less on vacation travel to save more for our children's education fund, we are making a financial decision that is consistent with that value. The trick is to overcome the emotional temptation to spend in the short term rather than save money to support one of our long-term values.

Second, you can choose, whenever possible, to earn money by working for, or investing in, organizations that offer worthwhile products or services. When it comes to the social value of products, not all businesses are created equal. For instance, if I had a choice, I'd rather work for a company that makes computers than one that makes cigarettes.

Third, you can use some of your money to support worthwhile causes. If you consistently make wise financial choices about spending, saving, and investing, it's likely you'll accumulate money beyond what is required to meet your basic needs. You can then use some of those discretionary funds to help charitable, civic, or educational organizations of your choosing.

Economists and financial experts have known for a long time that people often don't do the logical thing when it comes to their money. They've emphasized the need to change the way we behave around money. But there has been precious little practical advice about exactly how to change our financial behavior so we consistently act in our best interest. In the past, I've needed help in this area as much as anyone. Though I have been a successful and well-compensated executive in the financial services industry, I haven't spent my whole life as a paragon of financial decision-making. The approach described in this book owes as much to my financial mistakes as it does to my professional accomplishments. For example, I know what it's like to come home to a cold, dark house because the utilities were shut off for lack of payment. (My wife, then pregnant, was not too thrilled with me that day.) I know what it's like to have a cash withdrawal declined because the IRS has put a levy on my bank account. And I know how foolish it feels to lose millions in an exciting but ill-conceived business start-up. Those missteps fueled my desire to understand the inner workings of financial decisions, and eventually to develop a system for reliably making good ones.

Over the last eight years, my company, the Lennick Aberman Group (LAG), has developed a highly effective approach to decision-making. Through our behavioral advice workshops, we've taught this approach to over a thousand financial advisers and their clients—people like you who want to make smart, values-based financial decisions. LAG's approach integrates financial planning basics with recent findings from the fields of neuroscience and psychology to help you achieve the physical, mental, and emotional state you need to make and implement smart, values-based financial decisions. This book is the first time that the financial decision-making system LAG teaches in its workshops has been made available to the general public. *Here are some highlights of what you will learn:*

- **How to put values in the forefront of your financial life.** It's hard to make values-based decisions if we aren't really clear about what our values are. Try this: In the next five seconds, name your top five values. Were you able to name at least five things you value? If you're like most people, you were probably able to name one or two. Five seconds may not seem like a reasonable amount of time for you to name your values. But your brain evaluates situations not in seconds, but in milliseconds. If your values aren't top of mind when you're making decisions, it's that much more likely you'll make choices at odds with what really matters to you. In this book, we'll take you through a process to help you identify your most important beliefs and values.

    But getting clear about your personal values is only the first step. You'll also learn a number of creative techniques to ensure that you keep values in mind when you are in the thick of a challenging decision-making process. For example, one young couple who had a shopping problem was able to curb spending and increase savings for their daughter's education after they put a small card in their wallets reminding them how much they valued her future education. Each time they reached for a credit card, that values message came out first. Once they reminded themselves of that value, they were less likely to make an unnecessary purchase.

- **How our brains get us into financial trouble.** Whenever we are excited by an investment opportunity or fearful about a market downturn, our primitive survival mechanisms take over and the rational parts of our brains don't operate the way they should. That leads us to make emotional decisions stimulated by outside events, rather than logical decisions based on the realities of our lives, our goals, and our values. In addition to emotional barriers, our everyday thought processes are contaminated with mental shortcuts that are meant to help us make decisions more quickly and easily, but that often backfire. You'll learn how to spot your emotional patterns and mental biases and keep them from interfering with sound financial decisions.

- **How to build a solid, values-based financial plan.** Many people avoid financial planning because it seems stressful, complicated, or, if professionally prepared, perhaps expensive. This practical and straightforward financial planning approach is based on the idea that the purpose of financial planning is to prepare you for the certainty of uncertainty. We can't predict the future; we can't know when markets will go up or down, and we can't know when job loss, illness, or death will strike us or those we love. But we can be prepared. We can do things to buffer ourselves and our families from unexpected events. We can also set long-term financial goals that are aligned with important personal values. Whether you have a lot of money or a little, this approach will ensure that whenever you need money, for whatever reason, you will always have a smart place to get it. Using the "Preparing for Uncertainty Decision Tree" you will be able to confidently put in place the essential elements of a sound, values-driven financial plan.

- **How a simple four-step process (the "4Rs") can dramatically increase your ability to make smart financial choices.** When you practice these steps regularly, you will actually retrain your brain to respond to financial opportunities and challenges in ways that are in your best interest. Instead of responding reflexively, based on emotions and mental biases, these four steps will give you the power to make consistently good financial choices aligned with your most important values and goals.

In addition to giving you the essential tools for making smart financial decisions on your own, *Financial Intelligence* will help you think through what kind of professional help you may need to accomplish your financial goals. If you have shied away from using a financial adviser in the past—perhaps because you worry that a financial professional is more interested in lining his pocket than yours—this book will show you how to hire a financial expert dedicated to helping you achieve your most important life goals.

WHY I WROTE THIS BOOK

I wrote this book to help people make the best possible financial decisions for themselves and their families. Whenever people use the approach you'll learn in this book, their financial lives improve. But more than that, every area of their lives improves. When we follow up with behavioral advice workshop participants about how they are using the skills they learned in the workshops, nearly everyone tells us how this approach has changed not only their financial lives but also their personal and professional lives. It turns out that this approach to decision-making works well when applied to any area of life, not just finances. One mother taught the process to her 20-year-old son, a college student, to help him figure out what he wanted to do with his life. A talented but overloaded technology manager used the approach to curb his short temper. A successful salesperson used the approach to help him communicate better with his wife. And a medical research director used the method to plan how to juggle all the demands of her professional and family life. Behind each financial success story you will read in these pages, there are many more instances of how people are using this approach to lead better lives overall.

Ultimately that is the purpose of the book: To make smart decisions about money and about every aspect of your life that is important to you. Because *money* matters only when money helps you live a *life* that matters. I'm confident that this book will help you do just that.

1 | *Money on Your Mind*

John Sanders woke up in a sweat after a restless night tossing and turning. It was the morning of October 10, 2008, one day after the Dow Jones Industrial Average (DJIA) tumbled nearly 680 points. It was one of the largest single-day point losses ever, wiping out hundreds of billions of dollars in market value. The credit markets were frozen and the United States House of Representatives had created a crisis of confidence by voting down a $700 billion bank bailout plan.

John and his wife Susi were in their mid-50s and hoping to retire in about five years. The previous night before dinner, John had gone on Morningstar's Web site to survey the damage to their retirement accounts. Looking at a sea of ugly red arrows, John felt his heart pounding. His hands were shaking. He could barely sit still on his home office desk chair. Susi called him for dinner, but there was no chance he could swallow even a bite. "We can't afford to lose any more money than we already have this month," John decided. He clicked over to his retirement funds company, and transferred all his equity mutual funds into his linked money market account.

During the next few days the market rebounded. On October 13, the market rose 936 points—the largest single point gain in history—closing at 9,389.61. Driven by excitement and arousal, John made another quick decision, and bought back in to the funds he had abandoned only three days earlier, thereby locking in nearly $100,000 in equity losses. The market rebound was short-lived, and by March 9, 2009, the DJIA had fallen to 6,547.05, down more than 25 percent from the beginning of the year. If John had either stayed in the market and never sold, or stayed out of the market once he sold, John's investment value would have been higher than it was by March 9, 2009.

Where did John go wrong? He reacted to the stock market dive as if it were a matter of life or death. He made several quick decisions in October 2008 driven by fear and greed. If a car had been about to crash through his home office wall on October 9, 2009, John's quick reflexes could have saved the day. But as unpleasant as the decline in the stock market was, it wasn't an emergency. In fact, the U.S. markets were, as always, closed for the night, and nothing more awful was going to happen before they reopened the following morning. John had plenty of time to think through what he should do about the sorry state of the stock market. And since he and Susi weren't planning to retire for at least five years, nothing in their current life was in jeopardy because of the stock market's performance during the previous days and weeks. But none of that reasoning made it into John's thought process, because John, like all of us, was hampered by a Stone Age brain. John's brain, like ours, was well-equipped to handle physical survival, but pitifully unprepared to deal with the challenges of today's complex financial environment.

YOUR STONE AGE BRAIN

In the last 30 years or so, new technologies have revolutionized the way we live our lives. High-tech tools have profoundly affected the way we interact with money: We get cash from the ATM, make purchases with credit cards, pay our bills online, and check the latest stock prices on our smartphones. But all this technological sophistication is masking two dangers. One, technology makes it easier for us to spend money impulsively. Money is available 24/7. Credit cards let us buy things even if we can't really afford them. Easy access to money, coupled with a culture that prizes material possessions, has created an epidemic of thoughtless and often catastrophic over-spending across all socioeconomic groups.

Another danger is that our current social climate of continuous technological advances creates the illusion that we humans are more advanced and sophisticated than we really are. It's true that homo sapiens are great at making new tools. But when it comes to decision-making, we're relying on an old-model brain. Our brains were optimized to handle the challenges of life 10,000 years ago. Our brains are still evolving, but they can't begin to keep pace with the societal, cultural, and economic changes of the last 100 centuries, let alone the last 100 years.

While the brain inside your head is only as old as you are, its structure and circuitry date back to prehistoric times. Scientists who study human evolution say that the human brain, which grew and changed dramatically over the course of millions of years, has not significantly changed in size, weight, or organization in the last 50,000 years. From that, we can suppose that our brains were ideally suited to dealing with the demands of the environment at least 50,000 years ago. If we knew what life was like for people who lived that long ago, we could understand what kinds of situations our brains are equipped to handle. Unfortunately, we don't really know anything about people's lives that far back in time. But, thanks to the work of archeologists and paleontologists, we do have a picture of what humans faced 10 to 20 thousand years ago. Around 10,000 BCE, humans were hunter-gatherers, that is, they found food either by hunting for wild animals or by gathering edible plants and flow-ers. It took about another thousand years or so for humans to figure out how to grow food by cultivating land and planting seeds. (And it took another 9,000 years to come up with supermarkets and Starbucks!) Humans who lived 10,000 years ago developed special-ized stone tools (hence the term "Stone Age") to help them build shelters and acquire food. They lived in small groups, often in dwellings constructed of stone and roofed with animal skins. They moved around a lot, most likely to find fresh sources of food. Stone Age humans' major challenges happened in the physical world: How to avoid getting eaten by a woolly mammoth, how to figure out whether a plant was edible, or how to protect their families from the elements or from unfriendly tribes out to steal their supplies. Their brains were wired to help our species survive, not make complicated investment decisions. As Dr. Richard Peterson, noted psychiatrist, hedge fund manager, and author of *Inside the Investor's Brain: The Power of Mind Over Money*, explains:

> If you're a tribesman in the Serengeti region of Tanzania, Africa, and you come across a mango tree, you want to get as many mangoes off that tree as you can before a lion shows up. In that scenario, greed and fear are good. Those emotions are essential to survival. Really extreme emotions keep you alive. The trouble is, when it comes to financial matters, there's nothing like the mango tree. The stock market isn't a mango tree full of mangoes. It's a completely different and unpredictable entity. But we deal with it as though it was that mango tree.
>
> While our neural programming is brilliantly organized to help us meet physical challenges, it's not built to handle contemporary challenges such as financial decision-making.[1]

BRAINOLOGY 101

To understand how we make financial decisions, or decisions of any kind, we first need to understand how the brain operates. The brain is divided into three major sections. In the outer layer is the brain's rational center, which handles complicated cognitive processes, such as objective thinking and rational decision-making. The brain's rational center is largely composed of an anatomical section of the brain called the cerebral cortex. In the middle layer of the brain is its emotional center, which processes emotions, motivations, and drives. The major anatomical component of the brain's emotional center is called the limbic system. Within the limbic system is the amygdala, which translates outside stimulation into specific emotions such as

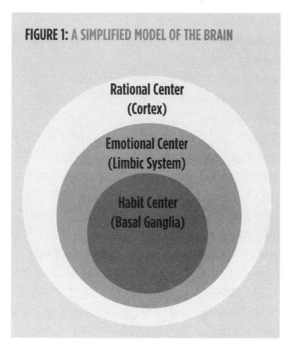

FIGURE 1: A SIMPLIFIED MODEL OF THE BRAIN

Rational Center
(Cortex)

Emotional Center
(Limbic System)

Habit Center
(Basal Ganglia)

fear or excitement. The inner part of the brain, the habit center, processes everything we do automatically without thinking. It includes not only habits, but also basic body functions such as breathing, circulation, movement, and sensation. The most significant anatomical part of the habit center related to financial decision-making involves the basal ganglia, which automatically seek out anything we recognize as rewarding, thus leading to the formation of habits. These three parts of the brain—the rational center, the emotional center, and the habit center—work together. They are connected to one another by neural circuits, that is, pathways that use special chemicals to send information back and forth among different parts of the brain.[2]

Here's an example of how the three parts of the brain are connected: Imagine you hear a rumor that almost all the jobs in your department at work will be eliminated. Within 12 milliseconds, what you heard activates the part of your brain that processes emotions and you feel frightened and anxious. Your emotional brain immediately sends a chemical message to your inner brain, which cues your heart to start beating faster and your breathing to become shallower. Meanwhile, it takes a sluggish 40 milliseconds for your outer analytical brain to get the message about the possible job eliminations—not nearly as quickly as your emotional brain. You try to figure out whether a job loss is likely, given that your company's profits are trending lower. You decide that the rumor is probably true, so your anxiety level rises, and your heart rate continues to beat rapidly. All of this has happened in a matter of seconds.

Now, suppose you heard about the rumor from someone who seems always to know what's going to happen. And suppose you've just made an offer on a new home. You start to panic. You're sure that you will lose your job. So you call your real estate agent and tell her that you must withdraw your offer. Three weeks later, instead of losing your job, you are offered a promotion. You now will earn several thousand dollars more per year than you had before. You call back your real estate agent and discover the home you dreamed of having has been sold to another buyer.

What happened to those connections between the three parts of your brain? Your emotions of fear and anxiety were so strong that they disabled the rational center of your brain. It's not that you *weren't* thinking at all, but that your strong feelings affected the *quality* of your thinking. The message that your brain's rational center received had already been "spun" by your brain's emotional center. What seems like a logical decision (I should withdraw my offer because I'm about to lose my job) is really pseudo-logic that justifies doing what you emotionally feel driven to do. Imagine what would have happened if you had made one call to someone in authority at your company, expressing your concern about a possible job loss. It's likely you would have been assured that you were in no danger of losing your job, and you might also have learned that good news was on its way. The one phone call you *did* make— withdrawing your offer to buy a new home—turned out to be the wrong call.

Why did hearing the rumor about a possible layoff cause such a lapse in judgment? Because the triggering event—the rumor—was *emotionally stimulating*. While the potential of a layoff was no doubt disturbing, when paired with a decision to buy a new home, the potential job loss became even more frightening. When we're in such an emotionally charged situation, our brains act *reflexively*: We do things automatically, without thinking clearly.

If our emotions are highly negative, they activate the brain's *loss avoidance* or *danger system,* a complex set of neural circuits that communicate across all three anatomical sections of the brain whenever we perceive threats or dangers in our environment.[3] If our emotions are highly positive, they activate the brain's *reward system,* a collection of neural circuits running across the three divisions of the brain that scans our environment in search of things we want.[4] When our reward system is highly activated (in the presence of highly positive emotions), it turns off our danger system. When our danger system is activated, it neutralizes our reward system. As far as our brains are concerned, there are no shades of gray: We are either excited and pursuing rewards, or we are fearful and trying to avoid danger. Perhaps you've had the experience of feeling so worried about something that it was impossible to enjoy a normally pleasurable event. That's because in the presence of either highly exciting or anxiety-producing financial situations, our rational brains are MIA. In the case of the layoff rumor, for instance, our anxiety and fear blocked our ability to make a rational decision to check out the accuracy of the rumor.

THE DANGER SYSTEM

The danger system is the circuitry in the brain that gets activated when we feel threats to our survival. Neuroscientists have not yet definitively mapped the brain anatomy of the danger system. However, it is believed to largely involve structures in the limbic system, including the insula, which registers pain or disgust, the amygdala, which processes emotions, and the hippocampus, which processes long-term memory. The danger system also is thought to include the hypothalamus, which secretes hormones that send messages to other systems in our body, including the endocrine system. When our danger system is activated, the whole body is involved. Our adrenal gland produces two chemicals: cortisol (often referred to as the stress hormone), and epinephrine (also known as adrenaline), which are secreted into the bloodstream, preparing our body to fight or flee the danger we are facing.

Cortisol gives us the energy to deal with a physical threat by increasing our blood pressure and blood sugar. Epinephrine prepares the body for action in emergency situations. It boosts the supply of oxygen and glucose to the brain and muscles, while suppressing non-emergency bodily processes. Some signs that your danger system is in charge: shaking, sweating, breathing quickly, or feeling panicky. But just because you don't feel any of those symptoms doesn't mean that your danger system isn't active.

THE REWARD SYSTEM

The reward system is the set of circuits in the brain that helps us identify and acquire things we want. It is made up of a bundle of neurons in the midbrain that send projections throughout the prefrontal cortex, affecting the rational processing ability of the brain. The neurons in the reward system communicate primarily by releasing a chemical called *dopamine*. When we see something potentially desirable (chocolate, an attractive person, a higher-paying job) our reward system turns on, motivating us to want this thing that has come to our attention.[5] What's interesting is how dopamine helps motivate us to go after what we want, by making us feel good. That's why dopamine is typically referred to as the pleasure chemical. Thanks to dopamine, we feel good when we anticipate getting what we want, and we feel good when we've gotten what we wanted.

Both reward and danger systems can be operating without our knowing it. That means we can be under the sway of emotions we're not consciously aware of, making decisions that we mistakenly think are objective.

PATTERNS IN THE BRAIN

When it comes to making decisions, there's a lot more to the brain than its reward and danger systems. Our brains also are wired to instantaneously detect patterns. This pattern-spotting skill has great value for our physical survival and well-being: A screech of brakes is often followed by a vehicle crash; overeating is often followed by indigestion. Running a few miles may result in feeling calm and happy. Such patterns are real, and they help us predict the future. If A happens, then B will soon follow. Therefore, I can make a decision to seek out something that will probably result in a positive outcome, or I can decide to avoid something that usually would result in harm. Recognizing those patterns can thus help us more efficiently avoid danger or secure rewards. When I hear the screech of brakes, I immediately scope out the best way to avoid the source of the noise. Because I want to feel good, I lace up my running shoes every morning and head out for a jog, usually without even consciously thinking about why I am doing so. But, as neuroeconomist Scott Huettel points out, "... in our modern world, many events don't follow the natural physical laws that our brains evolved to interpret. The patterns our modern brains identify are often illusory, as when a gambler bets on 'hot' dice or an investor bets on a 'hot stock.'"[6]

This predisposition to see patterns works against us when we are looking at situations that are, in fact, random and unpredictable. Most financial phenomena are not governed by predictable patterns. If the stock market goes up, we think it will keep going up. If the housing market is hot, we assume that will continue. If we've gotten a raise every year, we expect to see an increase next year. When we read about a mutual fund that has outperformed the stock market three years in a row, we buy into the pattern and sign up—even though a purely logical assessment of the situation would tell us that there is no reason to believe that something will keep happening just because it has been happening. In fact, if the past is a predictor of the future, then what it really tells us is that what goes up must come down, and vice versa. As Hersch Shefrin, behavioral finance pioneer and author of *Beyond Greed and Fear* points out, "Past performance is a great predictor of future expectations, not future performance."[7]

THE NEUROSCIENCE OF FINANCIAL DECISION-MAKING

John Sanders, whom we met at the beginning of the chapter, shows us how our brain's wiring reacts when we're in the throes of a highly charged financial situation. Given what was at stake for the

Sanders—their post-retirement comfort and security—the quality of John's decision-making was critical. Looking objectively at his situation, we realize that he had more than five minutes to make a significant decision about his retirement savings. But, because John is human, he was at the mercy of his brain's default wiring. His brain, like ours, is programmed on one end to detect and avoid danger, and on the other end to perceive and pursue opportunity. To ensure our physical survival, our brains are hypersensitive to perceived threats. When we sense danger, our brain's danger system activates. It immediately sets off a whole host of physiological changes that help us get away from the source of the danger. Our danger system turns our analytical centers off, as if to say, "You don't have time to figure out the nuances of this situation. Just get out of here!" It also turns off all nonessential bodily functions, including limiting blood flow to the hands and feet to minimize damage in case of injury. But even when we're not in physical danger, such as during a stock market crisis, our automatic danger response still kicks in with a flood of emotions that are better suited for escaping from a bear than dealing with a bear market. When we really are in a dangerous, life-threatening situation, we need a quick response. It saves us. But stock market volatility, while often emotionally painful, is not life threatening. So sacrificing the accuracy of our rational brains for the speed of our emotional brains begins to work against us.

A historical point drop in the Dow Jones Industrial Average will always get the attention of our brain's danger system. And once our brains are triggered by a scary external event, our emotional brains take over. That was the case for John Sanders. John was hostage to his emotional brain. He experienced all the physiological symptoms of a life and death crisis. John jumped the gun. Within a few minutes he had taken an action to deal with his perceived emergency. Except he *wasn't* in any immediate danger. He didn't need to do anything on the night of October 9, 2008. He had hours. In fact, he had weeks, even months, to plan a thoughtful response to the realities of a challenging financial environment.

If John had possessed full access to his rational brain, he would have recognized that, logically, there was no reason why he couldn't have enjoyed a tasty dinner and a restful night's sleep after that difficult October day. It made no logical sense to bail out on a big market downturn and jump in on a big upswing. But, like all of us who aren't trained in the skills of smart financial decision-making, John was stuck on emotional auto-pilot. His brain's danger system was in charge one day, and his reward system was in charge a few days later. And when one system—either the danger system or the reward system—is operational, the other is disabled. In both cases, his brain's limbic system (home of our brain's emotional center) hijacked his pre-frontal cortex (home of our brain's rational center). What wasn't affected was the part of his brain that houses automatic responses. So John's default mechanism under pressure was to respond to highly charged situations as he had always dealt with them in the past, whether that made financial sense or not.

CAN WE CHANGE OUR BRAIN?

Given the way our ancient brains are wired, how can we possibly make smart financial decisions under duress or in the thrall of an exciting opportunity? Fortunately, we can change the way our brains respond to financial situations. Though we're wired to behave in ways that can get us into financial trouble, our brains also have the capacity to create response patterns and new habits. Recent neuroscience research has revealed that the brain is "plastic." Neuroplasticity means that the brain can change. We can create new habits, so that when faced with challenging financial situations, we can respond in ways that are in our best long-term financial interest. With practice, we can undo our typical reactions to financial situations and establish new responses that activate the logical parts of our brains. And the first step to reprogramming our brains is to get in touch with the values we would like our financial decisions to reflect.

ENDNOTES

1. Richard Peterson, personal communication with Doug Lennick, April 28, 2008.
2. Adapted from Peterson, Richard L. 2007. *Inside the Investor's Brain: The Power of Mind Over Money*.

Hoboken, New Jersey: John Wiley & Sons. 23–25; and Zweig, Jason. 2007. *Your Money & Your Brain: How the New Science of Neuroeconomics Can Help Make You Rich.* New York: Simon & Schuster. 14–18.

3. Peterson, Richard L. 2007. *Inside the Investor's Brain: The Power of Mind Over Money.* Hoboken, New Jersey: John Wiley & Sons. 25–26.

4. Ibid.

5. Antoine Bechara, quoted in Zweig, Jason. 2007. *Your Money and Your Brain.* New York: Simon & Schuster. 64.

6. Quoted in Zweig, Jason. 2007. *Your Money and Your Brain.* New York: Simon & Schuster. 70.

7. Shefrin, Hersh. 2002. *Beyond Greed and Fear: Understanding Behavioral Finance and the Psychology of Investing.* New York: Oxford University Press.

2 | *Why Values Matter*

Texas retirees Dale and Amy Harbison are standing in front of a home that values built. More accurately, seven homes. In 2006, they personally financed construction of a quadriplex house and a triple house now occupied by seven single moms and their kids. These moms are enrolled in a program that provides free housing for their families while they pursue the training or education they need to get out of poverty. They don't pay rent, but neither do they get a free ride. The women need to work very hard, do well in school, take good care of their children, stay drug-free, and maintain their homes. Dale and Amy are too modest to mention what they spent on this ambitious project. They just say it's the best investment they ever made.

Jim Sudac and Dana More-Sudac, both in their mid-30s, live in Munster, Indiana, with their 2-year-old son Jack and their new baby, Sam. Jim sells wooden pallets for manufacturing companies, 100 percent commission based. Since Sam was born, Dana has become "semi-retired" from her job selling insurance. When they built their dream house a few years ago, they were careful to ensure that it wouldn't be one of the biggest on the block. They always add extra to their monthly mortgage payment. They put $250 into their mutual fund every Friday. They've thought about dropping their cable TV, but have decided that might be taking frugality a bit too far. They've made a point of not keeping up with the Joneses. "We save;" says Jim, "our neighbors consume. Now they're wondering how Dana can afford to cut back so much on her work."

What do these two very different couples, at different life stages and with different financial resources, have in common? Both couples are highly values-driven about how they use their money. The Harbisons are committed Christians who want to help the poor in a meaningful way. The Sudacs are highly focused on family and financial security. Oh, and the two couples have something else in common: They haven't always been paragons of values-based decision-making. They've made mistakes with their money, mistakes caused by the failure to keep values front and center.

Back in the 1980s, the Harbisons were lured by the prospect of making quick money through limited partnerships. They invested in quite a few of them—oil, gas, real estate, horses, and cattle. The investments tanked and the promised tax benefits were minimal. The Sudacs' only major lapse came a few years ago, when they walked into a Lexus dealership and drove out with a beautiful new car. Their financial adviser, who happens to be Dana's brother, Derek More, scolded them mightily. But they did keep the car, since the depreciation from selling it so quickly would only have compounded the mistake.

If there's a moral to the stories of these two couples, it is this: When we make decisions that are disconnected from our values, we usually come to regret them. When we put our money where our values are, we do well—financially and personally. This sounds so obvious, but few of us consciously and consistently align our financial decisions with our values. We let our emotions get the better of us, and end up with a too-good-to-be-true stock investment or a luxury car that limits our ability to invest in the things we really care about.

VALUES AND MONEY

Look in the dictionary and you may find this definition for the word "value":

1. Relative worth, merit, or importance: the value of a college education, the value of a queen in chess.
2. Monetary or material worth, as in commerce or trade: This piece of land has greatly increased in value.
3. The worth of something in terms of the amount of other things for which it can be exchanged or in terms of some medium of exchange.
4. Equivalent worth or return in money, material, services, etc.: To give value for value received.
5. Estimated or assigned worth; valuation: a painting with a current value of $500,000.
6. Denomination, as of a monetary issue or a postage stamp.[1]

You'll see that five of the six meanings of value are related to finances. So it shouldn't be too surprising that when we're thinking about financial matters, we're usually thinking predominantly about monetary value, such as how to make some more of it quickly, or how to avoid losing it. The antidote to this tendency is to focus on the first definition of value, meaning "relative worth, merit, or importance." Values are our life's priorities. They represent the things that are most important to us. Values are the boundaries within which we choose to live our lives.

Financial intelligence helps us support our deepest values: Money matters when we earn it by doing things that are worthy of our time and make a difference to others. Money is valuable, in the best sense of the word, when we use it to fund the things that matter most to us. There's an old saying, "Money can't buy happiness," meaning that having or spending lots of money doesn't necessarily make one happy. But there is a deeper sense in which money can buy happiness—if we use it to help us be the person we are meant to be. Of course, making values-based financial decisions is no guarantee that we'll become wealthy. But it will increase the likelihood that we'll have the financial resources we need to be financially independent, that is, not dependent on anyone else for our financial well-being. We'll have enough. We'll feel satisfied. We'll be using our money to live a meaningful life of our choosing. Arun Abey reinforces the importance of values-driven financial decision-making in his book with co-author Andrew Ford *How Much is Enough? Making Financial Decisions that Create Wealth and Well-Being:*

> Although more wealth can make a significant contribution to well-being, the real difference between the happy rich and the unhappy rich seems to be that the former see money as a means to an end, a contributor to the achievement of personal goals that are consistent with their personal values, rather than an end in itself.[2]

Minneapolis-based financial planner Steve Lear couldn't agree more. Steve devotes a lot of his time to service-based projects and programs because they satisfy his need for meaning. For example, Steve has been a volunteer on over 40 disaster recovery missions in the United States. Steve says they never fail to reinforce in his mind the importance of relationships relative to stuff:

> The things that have given me contentment are things like trips, nice meals with friends and family, participating in team sports, study groups, education, philanthropy, and volunteering. Philanthropy and volunteering are hobbies for me. I don't hear too many people saying my hobbies are philanthropy and volunteering, but they're mine. I'd rather have a nice meal with someone than a second home.

You'll hear more about the work Steve has done in helping young people develop financial literacy in the final chapter, "Sharing the Wealth."

YOUR LIFE IN THREE FRAMES

As important and satisfying as it is to make decisions based on values, aligning financial decisions with values doesn't come easy. There are numerous landmines: emotions, such as fear or excitement; mental biases, such as overconfidence in our financial abilities; and a brain that was built for hunting woolly mammoths, not riding the roller coasters of equity and real estate markets. In chapters to come, you'll learn skills to deal with all those obstacles to smart, values-based financial decision-making. But first, you'll need to think about what you want in your life, because that is the foundation for making your money matter. To fully understand how important it is to align financial decisions with values, it's important to take a step back and recognize that financial decisions are just one category of decisions you make in your life. Other categories may include decisions about what kind of job you'd like, where to live, whether to get married or have children, which doctor you'll visit, whether to join a health club, whether to cut your hair short, what time to wake up in the morning. A great number of supposedly non-financial decisions also have financial implications, but all decisions have a relationship to your values. Your life decisions, whether momentous or minor, are either consistent or inconsistent with your values. There are few, if any, values-neutral decisions.

So if you want to live a life consistent with values, it's helpful to see your life as the alignment of three frames: your *moral compass* (including your principles, values, and beliefs), your *goals*, and your *behavior*. Together, these three frames represent the *alignment model*. Alignment happens when each frame is consistent with the others. You are in alignment when the way you behave is consistent with the goals you've set for your life, and when the goals you've set are consistent with what you value most for your life.

For example, let's say one of your values is family, and one of your goals is to provide for your family whether you are alive or deceased. Your behaviors, then, might include buying life insurance to protect against premature death, and saving and investing money to provide long-term security in case you live a long and fulfilling life.

LIVING IN ALIGNMENT

This book focuses primarily on the alignment model as it applies to financial decisions. However, you'll get the most value from this book if you recognize that ideas and tools presented here can also be used to

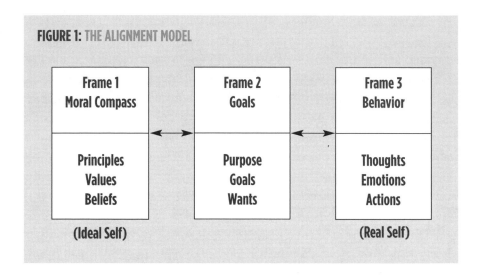

FIGURE 1: THE ALIGNMENT MODEL

Frame 1 Moral Compass	Frame 2 Goals	Frame 3 Behavior
Principles Values Beliefs	Purpose Goals Wants	Thoughts Emotions Actions
(Ideal Self)		(Real Self)

help you make the best possible life choices and achieve the best possible performance in *all* dimensions of your life. For example, if you value your family, there are many non-financial choices you can make to live in alignment with that value, for instance, deciding to spend quality time with your children or other family members.

New Jersey mathematics professor Rich Bastian, Ph.D., has three grandchildren who live nearby. Four days a week, he teaches classes and meets with students. Each Friday he spends time with one of his three grandchildren. He rotates their schedules so that at least once a month, each grandchild gets quality time with their granddad. In addition, Rich and his partner Louise host a weekly dinner for the kids, along with their mom and dad, Rich's daughter Jessica and her husband Erik. As you learn the skills for financial decision-making presented in later chapters, you'll discover that making financial choices and making other important life choices go hand in hand. Living in alignment is an approach to life, not just an approach to finances. You may not be making financial choices every day, but you'll be making countless other choices. The more all your life choices are in alignment with your values, the more fulfilled you'll feel as a whole.

Living in alignment is an ideal. It represents the person we would like to be at our best. Living in alignment may sometimes be difficult, but it doesn't require superhuman acts. It is about the day-to-day steps we take to do what we need to do to reach our goals. One of our colleagues used to avoid speaking engagements before large audiences, preferring to work with people one on one or in small groups. Eventually, he realized that he could not effectively communicate his values and beliefs if he limited himself to small group presentations. So he joined Toastmasters, the worldwide organization that helps people develop their public-speaking abilities. Our friend's desire to have a positive effect on the world led him to work on overcoming the anxiety of large group presentations.

Living in alignment is also not accidental. It requires doing things on purpose and for a purpose. Living in alignment is a two-part process. First, you build your own personal alignment model, by understanding what's inside each of these three frames:

- **Moral Compass**—What are your most important principles and values?
- **Goals**—What do you want to accomplish, personally and professionally?
- **Behavior**—What decisions will you make and what concrete actions will you take to achieve your goals?

Then, once you've built your own alignment model and know what should be in each frame, you work consciously and consistently to maintain alignment among your frames—simple, but as you might already suspect, far from easy.

FRAME 1: MORAL COMPASS

This frame contains the core moral principles and values that are the foundation of who we would ideally like to be as productive and fulfilled human beings. Principles and values overlap. The key difference is that principles are virtually universal: People everywhere tend to believe in their importance. These fundamental beliefs have been embedded in human society for so long that they are now widely recognized as universal. In my previous book *Moral Intelligence,* co-author Fred Kiel and I surveyed the research on universal principals and identified four primary principles held in common:

- Integrity
- Responsibility
- Compassion
- Forgiveness

It's no coincidence that financially successful people, no matter what their style or personality, all seem to follow the beat of the same drum. They listen carefully to the call of moral principles within all of us.

Values, on the other hand, tend to be an expression of what's important to us individually, and the values that matter most to me can be quite different from the values that matter most to you.

RADICAL RESPONSIBILITY

All four principles—integrity, responsibility, compassion, and forgiveness—are important, but the principle of responsibility is key to effective financial decision-making. Accepting responsibility for self, family, and community is at the heart of sustained financial health. Each of us is completely responsible for our financial well-being. This doesn't mean that each of us is responsible for becoming wealthy. But we are responsible for becoming financially independent, that is, not dependent on others for our financial health. We may never earn enough money so that work becomes optional, but we are responsible for making plans and choices that allow us to thrive, regardless of how much or little money we have. That's what makes it radical—the principle that financial responsibility is not related to income, but to our expectations of ourselves. Consider this example of radical financial responsibility: Gallup polling conducted at the end of 2008 during a historic recession found that only 36 percent of all Americans felt that they were "thriving," but almost 30 percent of the poorest Americans, those living on less than $24,000 a year, described themselves as "thriving." According to Gallup, "While the lowest-income Americans are still those most likely to be struggling, they did not see the stark increase in struggling in the first two weeks of November that those making over $24,000 did." What explains the difference between people who, despite their low incomes, still feel that they are thriving, while so many people earning three to four times as much report that they are struggling? Clearly, it's not about how much you earn. It is about your attitude about your life. Here is the secret that the "thrivers" have discovered. Responsibility is their guiding principle. They know that they are in charge. They know it's up to them to make sound decisions about financial opportunities that come their way. It's up to them to figure out in advance how to keep financial obstacles from turning into crises. And they do just that.

So the first step to financial success is to adopt responsibility as *your* guiding principle. Taking responsibility means recognizing that you can't afford to leave your financial well-being to chance events (such as winning the lottery), other people (such as your employer or your parents or the government), or broad economic trends (such as a bull market).

VALUES

Values differ from principles in that values are more personal beliefs about what is important to us as individuals. They are usually consistent with principles, and they allow us to put our own stamp on the meaning of the principles. For example, responsibility is a key principle, but our values help us choose how we individually express the principle of responsibility. We may value competence, challenge, or creativity. In each case, we can align our life choices with those values and with the principle of responsibility. Will I be responsible by using my competence, by taking on challenges, or by finding creative solutions to areas, such as work or family needs?

As we grew up, we learned a set of values, those qualities or standards that parents or caregivers considered important to our well-being and that of others. Over time, we came to adopt those values as guides to our own behavior. Families vary in the weight they place on certain values. They often emphasize a variety of values, such as helping others, creativity, knowledge, financial security, or wealth accumulation. Early in our lives, we typically adopt our families' values, and as we mature, we often add our own. By selecting, interweaving, and prioritizing our values, we define who we are—or at least who we want to be. Just as we recognize people by their physical characteristics such as hair color, height, or the way they laugh, we also come to know people by the values they embody. As we get to know friends or people with whom we work, we begin to recognize what means the most to them. Do they crave excitement, care about the environment, or seek status? We evaluate others based on how well our values mesh with theirs. You might value personal time for creative work more than social activities, while I might value relationships and family time more than professional recognition. We feel comfortable around people who share our most important values and often avoid those who don't. If you value financial security, for example, you may not like associating with people who seem to spend excessively.

DISCOVERING YOUR VALUES

What is the set of values that anchors you? How would you want others to think of you? It's no coincidence that financially successful people, no matter their style or personality, all seem to listen carefully to the call of moral values. Their values are important to them, and they consistently make decisions that are aligned with those values. To act in alignment with our values, we must deeply understand what they are.

Try this: In the next 30 seconds, say out loud your five most important values.

If you're like most, you may be stuttering or struggling to think. "Uh … family … financial security. Umm …" Our values are typically not top of mind. In fact, it's so hard to figure out our values that most values clarification exercises provide a list of common values for reference. Steve Pavilla, a noted personal-development blogger, offers a list of 374 values on his Web site. My company, the Lennick Aberman Group, created a pack of values cards, akin to trading cards, each of which names and explains a value. We've also produced special sets of values cards for kids and athletes. One of our clients, Seattle-based financial adviser Jim Bennett, described how he used the cards:

> The Values Cards have been a great tool for me to have conversations with clients, friends, peers, and family. These conversations lead to a discussion around goals and then around the alignment model. I have even been able to have a discussion about all this with my 8-year-old son.
>
> I use the cards to capture my clients' values and then tie these to their financial plan. I ask my clients, "If I see you living out of alignment can I call you out on this?" This has helped me better focus on my own values and goals and change my behaviors. All great stuff!

FRAME 2: GOALS

Scientists who study behavior tell us that humans have an innate need to make sense out of their lives. We constantly develop theories to explain why events happen as they do. We have an even deeper need to understand the meaning of our lives. How do our day-to-day events combine to create a coherent whole? What is the point of doing what we do? If we can begin to answer those questions, we have the beginning of our highest goal—our life's purpose. Not everyone develops and follows a life purpose. People who were seriously brain-injured or severely neglected or abused might lack the capacity to formulate a meaningful purpose. But most of us are hungry to make sense out of our lives, so we create goals. Everyone's life purpose is distinctively theirs, but each must be consistent with universal values, compassion, and forgiveness. Albert Schweitzer once said, "I don't know what your destiny will be, but one thing I do know: The only ones among you who will be really happy are those who have sought and found how to serve."

VALUES WORKSHEET
EXERCISE: WHAT ARE YOUR TOP FIVE VALUES?

Review this checklist of values and select the five that are most important to you. If you have an important value not on the list, use the blank spaces below to record other values. Don't rush through this exercise. Take some time to reflect on what really matters most to you.

☐ Adventure	☐ Autonomy	☐ Challenges	☐ Change
☐ Community	☐ Competence	☐ Competition	☐ Cooperation
☐ Creativity	☐ Decisiveness	☐ Diversity	☐ Ecology/Environment
☐ Education	☐ Ethics	☐ Excellence	☐ Excitement
☐ Fairness	☐ Fame	☐ Family	☐ Flexibility
☐ Freedom	☐ Friendship	☐ Happiness	☐ Health
☐ Helping Others	☐ Honesty	☐ Independence	☐ Integrity
☐ Leadership	☐ Loyalty	☐ Meaningful Work	☐ Money
☐ Order	☐ Philanthropy	☐ Play	☐ Pleasure
☐ Power	☐ Privacy	☐ Recognition	☐ Relationships
☐ Religion	☐ Safety	☐ Security	☐ Service
☐ Spirituality	☐ Status	☐ Wealth	☐ Work
☐ _____	☐ _____	☐ _____	☐ _____

Oprah Winfrey, who created one of the wealthiest entertainment empires in the United States, says this about purpose: "I've come to believe that each of us has a personal calling that's as unique as a fingerprint—and that the best way to succeed is to discover what you love and then find a way to offer it to others in the form of service, working hard, and also allowing the energy of the universe to lead you."[3] Perhaps you already know your life's purpose. Many of us have only a vague sense of it. Discovering your life's purpose usually takes a period of reflection. One of the best resources for clarifying your life purpose can be found in Richard Leider's book

PURPOSE WORKSHEET
EXERCISE: WHAT IS YOUR LIFE'S PURPOSE?

Take some quiet time to reflect on the questions below. Answering these questions can help you clarify the high-level meaning and direction that you would like your life to take. You may also find it useful to discuss your responses with a close family member or friend. Sharing your ideas with those closest to you can give you more confidence about what you are truly meant to do with your life.

1. **What are my talents?**

2. **What am I passionate about?**

3. **What do I obsess about, daydream about?**

4. **What do I wish I had more time to put energy into?**

5. **What needs doing in the world that I'd like to put my talents to work on?**

6. **What are the main areas in which I'd like to invest my talents?**

7. **What environments or settings feel most natural to me?**

8. **In what work and life situations am I most comfortable expressing my talents?**

Repacking Your Bags: Lighten Your Load for the Rest of Your Life.[4] Use the Purpose Worksheet to help provide you more insight about your life's purpose.

PURPOSE-DRIVEN FINANCIAL GOALS

Let's assume that you have a good sense of your life's purpose. Your life goals, including your financial goals, are the most satisfying when they are in service of your purpose. This is mostly a matter of common sense. Most people don't set financial goals arbitrarily. Few of us, for instance, randomly decide we want to acquire $2 million dollars. There's a reason we want that amount of money. There is something we want to accomplish by having that cool $2 mill. Our purpose is the major thing we want to accomplish in life. Our goals are more concrete things we'd like to accomplish to fulfill our purpose. The more aligned our financial goals are with our life purpose, the better off we'll be financially and the more likely we will be to actually accomplish our overall life purpose. An easy and powerful way to decide on your life goals is to use the "Widdy Wiffy" process Roy Geer developed, which he and I detailed in our book *How to Get What You Want and Remain True to Yourself.*[5] "Widdy Wiffy" is the phonetic pronunciation of the acronym "WDYWFY," which stands for "What Do You Want for Yourself?" The title contains a bias: Getting what we want is good. Our goals can be at the same time selfish and morally aligned. Getting what one wants for oneself is a rightfully selfish process provided that what one wants is in alignment with principles, values, and beliefs.

The importance of having specific goals is to ensure that what we actually do helps us create meaning out of our actions. Without goals, our ability to fulfill our life's purpose would be a matter of chance. Setting deliberate goals allows us to satisfy our wants in a way that is aligned with our moral compass.

Not only does your goal frame help you satisfy your financial wants within a moral framework, paying attention to financial goals also increases the odds that you will actually accomplish what you desire. If you don't work on your goal frame, there is a random occurrence of achieving your goals. Career expert David Campbell made that point famously in his book *If You Don't Know Where You're Going, You'll Probably End Up Somewhere Else.*[6] Apparently, it's not enough to have a set of goals in your head. You will boost your ability to achieve your goals when you write down your goals and your plans to achieve them. Why do written goals have such a positive effect? The most basic reason is that we tend to forget things. The physical process of writing helps our brains retain and recall the things we want to accomplish. When we write down goals, we have an opportunity to reflect carefully on what we really want and consider the best ways to accomplish them. When we record our goals, we can use our list as a reminder to stay on track. The process of writing down goals enhances our commitment and capacity to be responsible for the choices we make. We have all known highly intelligent individuals who never lived up to their potential. Goal setting will help you leverage the power of your moral intelligence to have a positive effect on your personal and financial well-being.

YOUR FINANCIAL (AND OTHER) GOALS

What exactly do you want for yourself—personally, professionally, and financially? What are your goals? The majority of us want to play our roles in life well. For example, most people who are parents want to be good at it. Even terrible parents want to be good at it. There are very few of us who don't care about how we perform. How many of you want to be part of a family that you are proud of? How many of you want to provide for your family's financial well-being? What do you have to do to accomplish that?

PUT IT IN WRITING

Whether you are developing new goals or reinforcing long-standing goals, writing your goals down will make them more real. Keep in mind that there are two kinds of goals. Some goals are a state-of-being goal, such as, "I have three children. I want to be a good father now." Another type of goal is a future-based goal, for example, "I want to retire in 10 years with a nest egg of $1 million." We recommend that you include goals of both types.

FRAME 3: BEHAVIOR

The behavior frame puts the "living" in "living in alignment." Your behavior frame represents what you actually do, including your thoughts, emotions, and outward actions. Your behavior frame takes your values and beliefs from Frame 1, and your goals from Frame 2, and makes them real. We cannot be financially successful unless we embrace principles and values, set clear goals, and act accordingly.

When we act stupidly, we give ourselves the benefit of the doubt, but our families, our colleagues, and our financial institutions do not. So keeping our financial behavior in alignment with our moral compass and goals is essential for financial success.

THOUGHTS

What makes thoughts part of our behavior frame? Psychologists recognize thoughts as a form of cognitive behavior. Thoughts profoundly affect our emotions and our outward behavior. And the trouble with thoughts is that they often pretend to be facts. Even when we think we are being logical and objective, often that's not the case. Most of us are biased about many things, and some of those biases get baked into our logic. For example, if I'm an avid fan of the football team that just made it into the Super Bowl, I might find it easy to justify spending a few thousand dollars to travel across the country to see the big game. In fact, I may unwittingly "underestimate" the cost of the trip, because I really want to go. And I might justify the expense even if it will add to my credit card debt or cause me to miss my daughter's birthday.

We also tend to rely on rules of thumb or mental shortcuts for making decisions. One of my rules of thumb might be, "Only invest in what I know." That might lead me to buy stock in Starbucks, because I stop there for coffee every day. But how effective is my rule of thumb? What are the consequences of taking a mental shortcut when making a financial decision? It means I have ignored a lot of important questions about the wisdom of my investment. The false sense of security provided by my rule of thumb may have kept me from questioning the significance of a slump in Starbucks' stock. Maybe I didn't question its strategy for dealing with new competitors (such as McDonald's now offering premium coffee) and the potential effect on future performance. And maybe I didn't ask about the relative advantages of owning stock in a single company versus managing risk by purchasing a mutual fund.

So always question your logic. It's really important to think through your financial choice. Even careful questioning won't mean you will always be right. There is no silver bullet for making optimal financial choices. But challenging your logic will make it more likely that you are making the most of all your cognitive and technical abilities.

EMOTIONS

Everyone has them, even the most rational and composed of us. Emotions have a strong influence on our view of financial situations and our response to them. That's because *your brain is hard-wired to encourage emotional decision-making.* As noted in the last chapter, when we're in the presence of a strong external event—say a big stock market surge or decline—the part of our brains that processes emotions gets the message first. In other words, the triggering event stimulates our emotional intelligence before it stimulates our cognitive intelligence. Our emotional intelligence sacrifices accuracy for speed. We act on a flood of emotions—fear (remember investors' panic after 9/11?) or excitement (remember the "irrational exuberance" of the 1990s?)—before the logical part of our brains gets a chance to evaluate the situation objectively.

Of course, the limitations of emotional decision-making don't just apply to stock investments, but to every decision we face that has financial consequences, such as job changes, geographical moves, real estate, or car purchases.

Keep in mind that emotions, in and of themselves, are neither good nor bad. They are simply emotions. But because strong emotions, whether positive or painful, can get in the way of effective financial decisions, emotions must be managed. The most financially successful people know how to regulate their emotional responses in a way that promotes sound decision-making.

ACTIONS

We all know that actions speak louder than words. Having a moral compass and admirable goals is worthless unless we do what it takes to make them real. In fact, failure to act in concert with our values and goals is worse than worthless. It is a failure of the core principle of responsibility. It does us harm. We lose money, and often we lose something more precious—others' trust and respect.

IN SEARCH OF ALIGNMENT

Now that you see the canvas inside each of your frames, how do you keep your frames aligned? Most people agree that the notion of living in alignment makes sense. If that's true, then why is living in alignment so hard? Why is it so difficult to make financial choices that support our values and goals? Why is it so hard to behave in ways that serve our financial self-interest? In the next chapter, you will begin to discover the secret to living in financial alignment—financial intelligence.

ENDNOTES

1. From Dictionary.Com Web site: http://dictionary.reference.com/browse/value?qsrc=2888.
2. Abey, Arun, and Andrew Ford. 2009. *How Much is Enough? Making Financial Decisions that Create Wealth and Well-Being.* Austin, Texas: Greenleaf Book Group Press.
3. Winfrey, Oprah. 2002. *O Magazine* (September).
4. Leider, Richard. 1995. *Repacking Your Bags: Lighten Your Load for the Rest of Your Life.* San Francisco: Berrett-Koehler Publishers.
5. Lennick, Doug, and Roy Geer. 1989. *How to Get What You Want and Remain True to Yourself.* Minneapolis, Minnesota: Lerner Publications Company.
6. Campbell, David. 1990. *If You Don't Know Where You're Going, You'll Probably End Up Somewhere Else.* Notre Dame, Indiana: Ave Maria Press.

3 *Planning for Uncertainty*

Sunday, February 25, 1996, was a typical Sunday for my mom and dad as they drove to church from their home in tiny Clements, Minnesota, to Redwood Falls, 11 miles away. On the drive, they chatted about their children and grandchildren, and about how happy they were that it was a bright, sunny day and that it wasn't snowing for a change. My mom teased my dad about the tie he had chosen to wear that day. They came to a stop sign at a highway. My dad stopped, and then started through the intersection. He didn't notice a car that was moving fast and headed toward them on the intersecting highway. The other car smashed into my parents' car on the passenger side, where my mom sat. First they were taken to the local hospital. My mom was in such bad shape that she was then air-lifted to a Minneapolis hospital 110 miles away. My wife and I rushed to the hospital, where my sister was already waiting and we were told that my mom needed surgery. Without surgery, they said, she had only a 3 to 5 percent chance of survival. With surgery, the doctors assured us, mom had a 95 percent chance of survival. A no-brainer. I signed the authorization for her surgery without a second thought. My mom died in the recovery room. She was healthy in the morning and gone by night.

That experience vividly brought home to me the certainty of uncertainty. I was rudely reminded that two things are true. One: We all will die. Two: We don't know when and how. But because we are uncertain about the second, we try to ignore the first. And that's the situation that many of us put ourselves in financially. Because we don't know when or how things will happen, we try to kid ourselves that they won't happen. We simply don't think about it. In the words of *Gone with the Wind's* heroine, Scarlett O' Hara, "I'll worry about that tomorrow."

When my mom died, my dad and my sister and my own family had no time to prepare emotionally. But eerily, my mom seemed to have prepared for her death. It's not that she expected to die that particular Sunday, but she did prepare for the certainty that she would die sometime. She didn't leave loose ends. She constantly nurtured her relationships. She made sure that her children, husband, daughter-in-law, grandchildren, siblings, and all her relatives knew they were loved. She was on top of all her responsibilities at work and at home. Everything was in its place. She was at peace with her God.

Like my mom, we all need to prepare for those predictably unpredictable events. Preparing for the certainty of uncertainty is the essence of the Smart Money Philosophy, the financial planning approach presented in this chapter. In addition to preparing us financially for life's twists and turns, the Smart Money Philosophy has two added benefits: By planning ahead, we are better able to ensure that our values will be put into action. When we plan, we have better access to our rational brains, and we're less likely to make ill-considered, emotionally driven decisions. And by putting our plans in writing, we have a concrete reminder of the financial strategies that we've decided will support our values and goals. Reviewing our plans regularly can reinforce our ability to maintain alignment with those values and goals, making it less likely we'll make impulsive financial decisions in moments of fear or excitement.

WHAT CAN'T YOU KNOW?

When it comes to life events and their financial implications, there are countless uncertainties. There is so much that we can't predict, no matter how smart we are. To be prepared for such unpredictable events, we must first understand *what we can't know.*

You can't know when your life or that of a family member will be significantly changed. No one knows when they or a family member will be struck with a serious illness, disability, or even death. You can't know when a new family member might be conceived and how expensive it will be to raise and educate that child or subsequent children. You can't know if your child might suffer from a learning disability or be blessed with one-of-a-kind talent, either of which might have financial implications.

You can't know what's going to happen with the overall economy. This includes economic factors such as inflation, employment, interest rates, the price of oil, GDP, and so on. Let's discuss a few examples from 2008 and 2009. You couldn't know that the price of oil would go to $145 a barrel in July 2008. Nor could you know that, two months later, it would be trading under $100 a barrel. Or that, even with a large drop in oil price, the price of gas would still be 60 percent higher than the previous year.[1] You couldn't know that unemployment would be at a 25-year high in August 2008, eventually exceeding 10 percent by the end of 2009.[2] You couldn't know that consumer inflation would hit a 17-year high in August 2008.[3] And you couldn't know how any of that would affect your job security, your salary, or your family's expenses for basic needs.

You can't know what's going to happen in the real estate market. For most Americans, the lion's share of their net worth is the equity in their houses. Given that roughly two-thirds of United States residents own their homes (or are mortgage holders), the majority of us are deeply involved in the real estate market. It's a fact that values of homes go up and down. There's no way to know exactly how much or when, but the last 20 years should have taught us that the strength of real estate markets can vary widely depending on time or region. For several years prior to 2006 there were four real estate markets that people believed could not go down: Florida, California, Arizona, and Las Vegas, Nevada. Those four regions are the ones that were hardest hit by the steep housing decline of 2007 through 2009.[4]

You can't know what's going to happen to the stock market. You couldn't know that the DJIA would reach 14,164 on October 9, 2007, and then fall by March 9, 2009, to 6,547, down almost 54 percent in fewer than 18 months.[5] You couldn't know that a crisis in the credit markets in September 2008 would severely damage the bond markets and threaten your retirement savings, even those in seemingly safe investments such as money market funds. What will happen to future financial markets? Will they go up? Will they go down? You just can't know with certainty. But I predict the answer is yes. It will go up and it will go down.

You can't know when your employment will be disrupted. You can't know whether your company may experience financial difficulties or be acquired by another business. You can't know whether your expertise will become outmoded or outsourced. You can't know when your company will decide to lay off employees, or whether your boss will decide you're not measuring up to his or her expectations.

SO, WHAT *CAN* YOU DO ABOUT WHAT YOU CAN'T KNOW?

At times, it can feel overwhelming to focus on all the sources of uncertainty in our lives. In the short term, it may seem easier to deny all the uncertainties that may affect us. It may seem easier not to think about things that *might* happen to us that might cause us harm. But, if we deny the certainty of uncertainty, most of us will at some point in our lives be faced with a stressful, perhaps even catastrophic, financial situation *that could have been avoided or mitigated.* Perhaps the triggering situation could not have been prevented, but the negative financial consequences could have been minimized.

What if, instead of burying our fear of those uncertain future events, we embraced the truth of uncertainty? What if we used the certainty of uncertainty to motivate us to create financial security and independence for ourselves and our families?

If you are willing to "reframe" uncertainty from a negative to a positive, you can prepare yourself financially for the certainty of uncertainty. That's not just a concept. In this chapter, you will learn a proven process for preparing for the certainty of uncertainty, a method that I developed over 30 years ago as a young financial adviser. This method, the Smart Money Philosophy, has created financial independence for me and thousands of people. I've taught this approach to thousands of financial advisers, who have used it to help their clients meet their financial goals of security and independence. I call this the Smart Money Philosophy because the plan is based on the idea that the best way to prepare for the certainty of uncertainty is to set things up so that, no matter what happens, you will be okay financially. When you follow the Smart Money Philosophy you cover all your bases, so whenever you need money you will have a smart place to get it.

KEY ELEMENTS OF THE SMART MONEY PHILOSOPHY

The essence of the Smart Money Philosophy is that you take steps to prepare yourself for a few basic but profound life scenarios. The Smart Money Philosophy prepares you for a long life or a short life, for good health or bad health, and for good times or bad times. It offers a clear and simple framework for making financially smart decisions and moving toward financial independence. The Smart Money Philosophy includes a step-by-step process for financial planning that you can use on your own or with the support of a financial professional. Because many people's financial situations are complex, I recommend that if possible, you engage the services of a financial professional. Chapter 9, "Calling in the Experts," provides a wealth of information on how to go about finding a trustworthy and competent financial adviser. However, the Smart Money Philosophy does not require that you use complex financial instruments, nor will it cover every possible financial scenario. The Smart Money Philosophy will help you figure out basic financial strategies, such as protecting your financial worth by diversifying your investments. Simply put, diversifying your investments means not putting all your financial eggs in one basket. Diversification helps you minimize the risk that some investments may not perform well by employing multiple kinds and classes of investments, such as cash equivalents, bonds, stocks, real estate, and so on. The Smart Money Philosophy will also tell you what to do—or not do—when you need money. You can make your Smart Money Plan as complicated as your circumstances warrant, but the beauty of the Smart Money Philosophy is that you don't need to get involved in sophisticated investments or complicated wheeling-and-dealing in order to achieve and enjoy financial independence. The Smart Money Philosophy will help you put in place a powerful Smart Money Plan that includes three key elements: saving money, diversifying your assets, and managing uncertainty risks.

Recognize that you *must* save money. If you want to be certain you'll have more money, you must save. *You must save money to have money.* There is no escaping that fundamental rule of the Smart Money Philosophy. You can never know with certainty that you won't need money. Therefore, there is no way to avoid the need to save. If there is one lesson learned from the "Great Recession" that exploded in 2008–2009, it is this: You cannot rely on credit cards or home equity as sources of cash to make desired purchases. Before the housing bubble began to burst in 2006, many people mistakenly thought that they didn't have to save. Real estate values kept rising, and banks were often aggressive about offering home equity lines of credit (HELOCs) that made it easy for people to turn their home equity into cash. Then home property values deflated, and as of 2009, were still declining. Many people now owe more on their homes than they are worth. Whether during good times or bad, it's a mistake to treat your home as a piggy bank. A generation ago, people knew they had to save money and that they needed to keep on saving money, no matter their age. My dad grew up during the Great Depression. When he died in 2009 at age 84, he was still saving money.

No matter what, find a way to spend less than you earn, so that you can put money aside for future needs. Establish a habit of regularly saving money, for example, setting up an automatic deduction from your paycheck or checking account or an automatic deposit into your 401(k) plan.

Put your investments in a variety of financial instruments. Develop the discipline and habit of diversifying your investments by

placing money in varied instruments. To help you make smart decisions about where to make investments, you may choose to consult
with an ethical financial planner or take advantage of free online
planning tools.[6] Having money in different places ensures that whenever you need money, and for whatever reason, you will have a smart
place to get it. So begin by regularly putting money into instruments
that have no risk at all, such as savings accounts or money market
accounts. You can also systematically buy government bonds, which
are guaranteed by the government that issues them. Despite recent
financial crises, it is unlikely that the U.S. government is going to go
out of business.

To prepare for retirement, invest money in a tax-deferred retirement plan such as a company sponsored 401(k) or an IRA (individual retirement account.) To help fund children's educational expenses, you can set up special college savings plans that include mutual
funds. You can also buy stocks, bonds, or mutual funds outside of any
special plan.

When making decisions about how to save and invest your
money, avoid the temptation to put all your money in any financial
instrument that is currently performing at a high level, for example,
a top-performing mutual fund or a real estate investment in a hot
market. Like Newton's apple, "What goes up, must come down." A
high-performing fund this month can crash and burn next month.
This advice may sound like a no-brainer, but it bears repeating, since
so many people are seduced by the prospect of making a lot of
money in a short time. A trusted and trustworthy financial adviser
can also be a big help here.

**Use insurance to transfer some of the risks of uncertainty to
someone else.** Most people think of diversification only in terms of
financial instruments such as stocks and bonds that they hope will
grow in value over time. But it's wise to think of diversification more
broadly to include allocation of some money into insurance products
that can help reduce uncertainty risks. "Investing" in insurance products is a powerful way to preserve assets and ensure that you and
your loved ones won't have to deal with life crises such as disability

or premature death by tapping into financial assets at a bad time, or by spending more money to deal with a life crisis than is necessary. Unfortunately, many people don't fully appreciate the importance of insurance as part of a financial diversification strategy. But take this example: In most states, you can't drive a car without car insurance. Everyone understands the simple idea that if you have a car accident, the costs of repairing vehicles and treating injuries can be enormous. The government therefore requires that we have a way to pay for those potential costs. It's ironic that we don't apply that simple logic to other possible life events. Life crises can be massively expensive. That is why insurance is so important. When we buy insurance, we transfer some of the financial risks of uncertainty to others, that is, to insurance companies.

- You don't know when you'll get sick or injured and need health-care, but if you have health insurance, you can greatly reduce uncertainty about how much you will have to pay to get treatment for a major health problem.
- You don't know if an illness or injury will happen, but you can transfer the risk of being unable to work to an insurance company that offers disability insurance.
- You don't know if a disability will make it impossible to care for yourself, but you can transfer the financial risk of needing care (for example in an assisted living facility or nursing home) by using long-term care insurance.
- You don't know when you'll die, but you can transfer the financial risk of dying early to a life insurance company, thus providing funds to support your loved ones after your death.

MAKING YOUR OWN SMART MONEY PLAN

In this section, you'll be guided to create the basics of a Smart Money Plan. You already know that you're responsible for your financial well-being and that the best way to prepare for the certainty of uncertainty is to save and invest money, as well as obtain appropriate insurance to cover predictably unpredictable life events. But how do you figure out how much money you really need? Ultimately the answer to that question is up to you. But I recommend that you aim for saving enough to be financially independent. Financial independence is sometimes thought of as freedom from the need to work. However, a more realistic definition is that financial independence is freedom from being financially dependent on anyone else. For some, financial independence can mean that you have enough income from your savings and other assets that you do not have to work, and that income will come to you for as long as you need it.

Because you don't know with certainty how long you will need to have income, your plan for saving and accumulating assets ideally will be designed to keep generating adequate income indefinitely. I recognize that not everyone will be able to accomplish this goal. But even the act of setting financial goals, and taking steps to achieve them, will dramatically increase your financial security.

HOW MUCH DO YOU NEED?

How much you *really* need depends on how much income you believe is required to support your desired lifestyle. If someone said, "I will pay you enough money each month so you don't have to work ever again if you don't want to," how much would that be? For some people, the answer would be more than they make now. For others, it would be the same income they're making from their current jobs. Still others would happily accept a reduction in income, for instance 60 percent of what they earn now, if it meant they could quit working. So think about how you would answer that question. Do you want or need to replace all the income you are currently making in your job? Do you think you would be happy with less? Do you want more income than you currently make in salary to pursue your dreams?

Since this isn't a fairy tale, it's highly unlikely that someone will wave a magic wand and release you from the need to work. Keep in mind the key principle of financial independence: You are responsible. One way or another, you will be creating your own financial independence.

SMART MONEY PLANNING GUIDELINES

Financial Aspirations. Smart Money planning works backward. That is, it's helpful to decide how much money you need or want on an annual basis to accomplish your financial and personal goals. When I first created the Smart Money Philosophy back in 1975, I wanted to be prepared for all the possibilities, including premature death, disability, and bad economic times. I wanted to become free from the need to work, even though I imagined I would always want to work. As a first step toward financial independence, I looked at what savings I had at that time, and it was pretty close to zero. So I knew I had to start from scratch to have a financially secure life. I began by defining what amount of annual income would allow me to be financially independent. I decided that if I had $15,000 a year coming to me from my various assets, I would become free from the need to work. (Remember, this was in the mid-1970s.) I calculated that I would need to accumulate $250,000. If I could earn a 6 percent annual return, I would receive $15,000 a year without tapping into the $250,000 I would ideally accumulate. So I began a systematic savings and investment program. Even as a young man, I understood the reality of life's uncertainties, so I created the planning framework detailed below:

- **Life** includes two main events: your physical life and your death. Your physical life ends when you die, but your financial life goes on beyond your death. That's because most of us leave behind some expenses, and often loved ones who need our financial support, or to whom we want to leave a financial legacy.
- **Health** involves being *healthy* or *not healthy*. Your health status may or may not affect your ability to work, or may affect your ability to generate income to varying degrees.
- **Work** involves either *working, working less than we desire,* or *not working.*
- **The Economy** may be either *strong* or *weak.* The strength of the economy can have varied effects on your financial status

depending on the particulars of economic conditions, your life, health, employment, and personal financial assets.

The Smart Money framework begins by systematically planning for worst case scenarios before moving to more desirable life scenarios.

SMART MONEY PLANNING SCENARIOS

- **Death.** Most people agree that untimely death is the worst case scenario, both financially and personally. So plan for death first. Determine, for instance, how much income or money your loved ones would need if you died suddenly. Then compare that with the income currently being generated by your existing capital and assets. If there is a gap, buy enough life insurance to cover that gap. That ensures your family will have a smart place to get money in the event of your death.
- **Life.** The financial needs you have during your physical life will vary depending on your health, your ability to work to gain income, and the varying nature of the economy. The major planning scenarios appear below:

     IIA. Alive but Not Healthy. A large percentage of people will experience the need for some significant medical treatment at some point in their lives. One trip to the emergency room with a child's broken bone can severely strain finances. That's why health insurance is so important. It's also very expensive, because so many people make claims against their health insurance. There are additional not-healthy scenarios that you need to plan for.

     IIB. Not Healthy and Unable to Work. How much income would you need if you suddenly became unable to work? Compare that with the income you could generate from your existing capital and assets. If that is not sufficient to meet your needs, you should purchase long-term disability insurance.

     IIC. Not Healthy and Not Able to Care for Oneself. As you age, the risk of needing some kind of long-term care rises. According to one study, 37 percent of people who died at age 65 spent some time in a nursing home, while 71 percent of those who died at 95 years of age or older had spent time in a nursing home.[7] It's important to consider how you would pay for nursing care, assisted living, or at-home healthcare if needed. All such care is expensive. If you do not have enough reserve capital and assets to pay for such care, it's important to purchase long-term care insurance.

IID. Alive and Healthy and Working.

Planning for Difficult Times. When the economy is weak and the stock market and/or real estate markets are falling, it's important to have access to a variety of sources of funds, including instruments that perform well when the economy is struggling. These include cash, cash equivalents, fixed assets (instruments that have a fixed principal value such as a guaranteed annuity), fixed income assets, and hard assets such as gold. You need a smart place to go for money to fund both positive and negative events, such as job loss, vacation, college tuition, etc. Cash and cash equivalents may have changing interest rates but the underlying value is fixed. Unlike cash, fixed income investments such as corporate, municipal, or government bonds will have fluctuating value, but the income is fixed and therefore will continue to provide a specific amount of income no matter what is going on in the economy. Cash is especially useful for immediate needs, because it's available without penalty. Fixed income investments are useful because they provide a fixed income. Precious metals such as gold can also be a smart place to get money during bad times. As we saw in the last decade, investments in precious metals often perform well when other investments, such as stocks or real estate, are declining. Figuring out how much of your total assets should be in cash and fixed income instruments or precious metals is both an art and a science. The concept is straightforward, but the nuances can be complicated. If you are a highly financially knowledgeable investor using the Smart Money Philosophy, you can accomplish a lot on your own. But most smart investors don't go it alone. They rely on financial professionals to help them identify and evaluate sophisticated options that will protect them in poor economies.

Planning for Good Times. When the economy is strong, equity instruments such as company stocks and mutual funds of stocks tend to increase substantially in value. Participating in the stock market can help you reach financial independence more quickly, because on average over time, stocks perform better than fixed instruments such as bank CDs or government bonds. If you need money when the economy is strong, then selling equity assets (for example stocks) that have appreciated can be a smart way to get it.

A SMART MONEY EXAMPLE: PAYING FOR COLLEGE TUITION

My son Alan went to college at a time when the stock market had been on an upswing. Because I had invested in the stock market for years, I had a smart place to go for tuition money. I sold stocks whose value had gone up since I had bought them. When my oldest daughter Mary started college in 2003, my stock investments had been pummeled. Had I sold stocks to pay for her tuition, I would have taken losses. But since I also had access to cash, I had a smart alternative: I paid her tuition in cash. When my younger daughter Joanie started college in 2006, I used a combination of stocks that were profitable to sell and cash.

Like stocks, real estate investments are also equity investments, and depending on the nature of the investment, one might earn rental income or capital appreciation in those times when real estate values are rising. Someone once said, "We can't create more land, but we are adding more people, so it stands to reason that over time real estate is an asset that will appreciate."

ADJUSTING YOUR SMART MONEY PLAN

As you continue to save and invest money, you may need less coverage in some insurance plans than you did earlier. At that point you may discover that, even if you *could* get by with less insurance, reducing your level of coverage may not be a smart financial move.

Continuing to use insurance to transfer risk to someone else can be less expensive than shouldering the risk on your own (even if you can afford to do so). Every year or so, review your financial picture and determine whether anything has changed significantly enough that you want to adjust your financial goals or actions. This process should always be done while considering your values. Remember that I started out wanting the lavish sum of $15,000 a year. As my family grew and living costs rose, I increased the amount I needed to be free from the need to work. Your needs and wants may increase—or decrease—over time. You can always adjust any action. With the recent economic downturn and market volatility I increased my life insurance because my net worth had gone down and I could not be certain it would recover before I might die. My own values that influenced my insurance decisions included *family, wisdom,* and *health.* I value family. I believe it's wise to be well insured, and because health is fragile I understand I can't count on the good health I have enjoyed all these years.

When I started my first job in the financial services industry in 1973, no one could know that we were in the first year of a flat stock market that would last for a decade. In December of 1972, the Dow Jones Industrial Average closed at 1020. At the end of 1982, it closed at 1047. Of course, it wasn't just a sluggish straight line to get those additional 27 points. During those 10 years, the market zigged and zagged. But those 10 years taught me, and others who experienced them, that you really can't predict what the market will do. In the next 10 years, your life will zig and zag, and you'll probably need money to help you manage all those twists and turns. Creating a Smart Money Plan is the foundation of your journey to greater financial fulfillment. You've prepared for all those events that can threaten your financial security. With that in place, you're ready to learn how to make smart financial decisions that reflect your values and make it possible for you to live a life of greater financial well-being and personal fulfillment.

ENDNOTES

1. Crude Oil Price History. New York Stock Exchange. 2010: www.nyse.tv/crude-oil-price-history.htm.
2. United States Bureau of Labor Statistics. 2009: www.bls.gov.
3. Consumer Price Index. United States Bureau of Labor Statistics. August 2008: www.bls.gov/cpi/home.htm.
4. Altos Research. "What is the Real Estate Market Doing Right Now?" www.altosresearch.com.
5. History of Dow Jones Industrial Average. December 2009: http://mdleasing.com/djia.htm.
6. The Financial Planning Association recommends this Web site for free financial planning tools: www.FPAforfinancialplanning.org/ToolsResources/Tools/.
7. Kemper, P., and C. Murtaugh. 1991. "Lifetime Use of Nursing Home Care." *The New England Journal of Medicine* 324 (February): 595–600.

4 | *Financial Intelligence*

When you meet Atlanta natives Joe and Alicia, they seem like an unusually happy couple. College sweethearts who married 15 years ago, they are proud parents of an elementary-school aged son and a daughter about to start high school. Alicia and Joe have good professional jobs. Together they earn nearly $150,000 a year. They own a beautifully decorated home in a desirable suburban neighborhood. They contribute to their companies' 401(k) plans. They have no credit card debt. They also have no emergency fund, and no college savings. Why? Joe and Alicia are spenders. Each was raised in a working class family where money was tight, and they feel they deserve to enjoy what they earn. Alicia is a recreational shopper with great fashion sense. She never met a Coach bag she didn't like, and she wouldn't be caught dead wearing costume jewelry—only real diamonds, please! Joe likes toys with engines, especially his BMW Z3, and a new Honda Nighthawk motorcycle paid for by dipping into a home equity line of credit. Despite the appearance of the good life, Alicia and Joe are not content. Lately they've been doing some soul searching. Without an emergency fund, they're one paycheck away from a financial crisis, despite their affluent lifestyle. And their kids are good students who they hope will eventually go to college. Alicia and Joe are beginning to realize that times have changed since they went to the University of Georgia on scholarships. Given the family's current income, their kids may not even qualify for financial aid. Education is one of their most important values, and they had always assumed they would pay for their children's college costs. So far, they haven't done a thing about it.

Joe and Alicia are a typical example of many American adults whose financial lives are out of synch with their most important values. In most respects, they're great people with good values. They value achievement. Because of that they worked hard to get through college and land good jobs. They value family—as demonstrated by how they value their marriage relationship. They've been happily married for a long time. They value financial security and are saving for retirement. But what about a financial safety net for today? If they were consistent in their behavior associated with financial security, they would be providing themselves with such a financial safety net. And what about being able to help their kids go to college? Is it that they don't care? From talking to Joe and Alicia, we know they do. What's happening is that the reflexive, emotional parts of their brains are disabling parts of their brains that might otherwise factor their values into their decision-making. They are impulse buyers, so instead of making decisions aligned with values related to family financial security and college education for their children, they are making decisions fueled by, among other things, past feelings of deprivation and the dopamine rush and immediate gratification of buying more "stuff."

Joe and Alicia have good values, but they lack *financial intelligence*. Financial intelligence *is the ability to make smart, responsible, values-based decisions with and about money in the face of competing and difficult-to-deal-with emotions.* Compare their story with that of another couple, Chuck and Lori Wachendorfer, who fortunately had the financial intelligence to make an important financial decision better aligned with their concern for their family's happiness. Chuck and Lori are avid skiers. They loved their dream house outside of Vail, Colorado. Perched near their favorite ski slopes, the beautiful contemporary boasted panoramic views of the Rocky Mountains. But by the fall of 2006, only three years after they'd settled in, the couple realized that they weren't living in the right place. Their growing children's schools, activities, and friends were all in or close to town. Transporting kids back and forth was inconvenient and even buying groceries and other needed household items was a hassle. But most important, their kids felt isolated from their friends. So they decided to move into town. Once they put the house on the market, they began to get offers that seemed to Chuck to be ridiculously low. Chuck wanted to turn down the latest lowball offer, while Lori wanted them to make a counteroffer. Chuck didn't want to settle for breaking even on the house sale. Lori wanted to move on quickly to get the family re-established in a place where they would all be happier.

Then Chuck had an epiphany. On reflection he realized that he had been thinking only about the financial aspects of the offer on their home, and not factoring in the value he placed on his family's happiness. He also realized that his financial assumptions were flawed. Because Chuck and Lori had sold each of seven previous homes at a sizable profit, Chuck had reasoned that they must make a profit on every house they sold. Chuck decided that was an unrealistic standard. When he invested in stocks, he did not expect to make money on every single stock; he expected to make money on the entire stock portfolio. So Chuck decided to think of their real estate investments as a portfolio: They may not make money on this particular house sale, but over time, they had made a lot of money on their portfolio of houses. Once Chuck had challenged his financial assumptions and put more emphasis on how much he valued his family's happiness, he was willing to make a counteroffer that led to a quick sale of the house.

As it turned out, fall of 2006 was the end of the housing boom in their area. Had Chuck and Lori waited for a higher offer, it probably never would have come. Within a few months, home values were sliding and houses comparable to theirs sat on the market for many months, selling for far less than the lowball offer that had initially frustrated Chuck, if they sold at all. And once Chuck and Lori sold their house, they were able to take advantage of the real estate decline when they bought their new house in town at a hefty discount from its original asking price.

Chuck and Lori's story had a happy ending largely because of their financial intelligence. Throughout their marriage, they've been deeply committed to the principle of responsibility. They know that they are accountable for all the choices they make—financial and otherwise. They also follow the two rules of financial intelligence:

1. Make financial decisions based on your values
2. Be prepared for the certainty of uncertainty

In addition, they've practiced the four key skills—the "4Rs" of financial intelligence: Recognize, Reflect, Reframe, and Respond.

Chuck, in particular, was able to use the 4Rs to overcome certain emotions and attitudes that were detrimental to his family's happiness. In the section that follows, you'll see exactly how Chuck used those critical skills, and as you proceed through the book, you will learn how you can develop those same skills.

HOW CHUCK USED THE 4RS

RECOGNIZE all the elements of the situation you are in. Stop whatever you are doing to take notice of everything you're thinking, feeling, and doing related to the financial situation you are in. Also pay attention to the objective facts surrounding your potential decision.

Chuck recognized that he was thinking they should make money every time they sold a house. Chuck recognized that he felt frustrated with the low offers on the house, and that he felt resistant to making a counteroffer, even though his wife wanted them to do so.

REFLECT on how you are interpreting your situation. What does the big picture really look like for you? What values are important to you and how should they influence your choices? What biases might be influencing your understanding of the situation you're considering?

Chuck's major insight was that he was not paying attention to his most important value, that of family happiness, in responding to the offer on their house. He was only paying attention to maximizing financial gain, and Chuck recognized that financial wealth is important to him, but not one of his top five values. He also discovered a bias in his thinking about financial investments: He expected to make a lot of money each time he sold a house, a standard that he would never apply to other financial investments.

REFRAME your ideas about the situation by stating the most positive yet still realistic outcome for the decision you need to make.

Chuck reframed his ideas about the house offer by deciding that he could accept a break-even offer because it would allow his family to be happier sooner. He also was able to reframe the break-even house sale as a financial success by seeing this house sale as part of a real estate portfolio that included his previous lucrative house sales.

RESPOND by making a decision that is consistent with your values and goals and takes the reality of your current situation into account.

Once Chuck had reframed his ideas about selling the house, he was able to negotiate successfully with the prospective buyer at hand. Chuck, Lori, and their kids were able to move sooner, and their lives became easier and happier.

HOW THE 4RS WORK

Chuck and Lori's story demonstrates the value of the 4Rs to financial

THE 4RS OF FINANCIAL INTELLIGENCE

▶ RECOGNIZE all the elements of your current situation and how you are interpreting (that is, "framing") your situation.

▶ REFLECT on the big picture and what matters most (your values and guiding principles).

▶ REFRAME (modify) what you are thinking and how you are describing the situation to yourself.

▶ RESPOND in a way that is consistent with your values, goals, and the big picture.

59

decision-making. But why are these seemingly simple skills so power-ful—and so necessary to making good decisions? The answer is that using the 4Rs rewires our brains to make the best possible financial decisions. As discussed earlier, most significant financial situations trigger emotional responses in the brain that override rational think-ing. Over time, these emotionally based responses to financial choic-es become habits. These habits are encoded in the brain in the form of neural pathways that increase the likelihood that we will respond in the same emotionally driven manner time and time again.

Fortunately, we've also learned that we have the power to change our response patterns in ways that allow us to make smarter financial choices. The 4Rs are designed to help us develop that power. By prac-ticing the 4Rs regularly, we create new neural pathways in the brain. By doing so, we establish new habits that, over time, replace our reflexive emotional responses with deliberate and reflective respons-es that take our values and genuine financial needs into account. The 4Rs help retrain our brains in a number of ways.

The 4Rs interrupt our brains' default responses to external financial situations.[1] When faced with highly stimulating events, the brain's emotional center typically disables the brain's rational center, thus provoking a fear or anger response that Daniel Goleman, author and emotional intelligence pioneer, labeled the "amygdala highjack."[2] Jeffrey Schwartz, noted psychiatrist and researcher in the field of neuroplasticity, has conducted research that explains the mecha-nisms underlying an amygdala highjack.

> The amygdala and the orbital frontal cortex are among the oldest parts of the mammal brain, remnants of evolutionary history. When these parts of the brain are activated, they draw metabolic energy away from the prefrontal region, which promotes and supports higher intellectual functions. The prefrontal region is particularly well developed in humans, and doesn't exist at all below the higher primates. Error detection signals can thus push people to become emotional and to act more impulsively: Animal instincts take over.[3]

According to Schwartz, in the process of shutting down our rational center, the amygdala leaves our habit center intact. Our habit center, which activates primitive physiological behavior and habitual unthinking responses to events, is now in charge of our decisions about complicated and potentially dangerous financial circumstances.

To prevent this chain of events, think of the 4Rs as hitting the pause button on our brains' programmed responses to highly charged financial situations. We may not always be able to prevent our brains from kicking up an emotional storm in the face of a financial danger or opportunity, but we can, by practicing the 4Rs, keep our emotional brains from hijacking our rational brains and setting our habit centers free to run the show. And, thanks to the brain's ability to develop new neurons and new pathways (neuroplasticity), when we hit the play button again, whatever we did during the pause contributes to changing our brain's actions going forward. To better understand the value of the pause, think about the times you've seen a trailing football team come back onto the field after halftime, acting like a completely different team. But the pause in itself probably wouldn't have been strong enough to propel the beleaguered team to victory. Something happened in the locker room that disrupted the team's losing pattern. The team had time to *recognize* its feelings of discouragement, and players' thoughts that they were going to lose. They also *recognized* that those thoughts and feelings had impaired their performance in the first half. They then reflected on the big picture and the realization that they were a talented football team, with the ability to win. With help from their coach, they were able to *reframe* their thinking about how to deal with themselves and access their best efforts in the second half. In essence, halftime was an opportunity to reprogram the team for a better response in the second half. Similarly, the 4Rs help us reprogram ourselves for a better *response* as financial decision-makers.

The 4Rs spur the development of new brain pathways that actually change the way we process information related to financial decisions. Extensive neuroscience research has left no doubt about the brain's ability to change. We can change our brains, but only if we deliberately try. As Jeffrey Schwartz explains, "Physical changes in the brain depend for their creation on a mental state in the mind—the state called attention."[4] That is why the 4Rs are effective in changing our brains—because they force us to pay attention to what we are doing.[5]

When we respond to a financial situation, we are usually reacting emotionally to stimulation from the outside in. The 4Rs give us the tools to respond to financial situations from the inside out. They change the power balance between the reflexive, emotional center of our brains (which sacrifices accuracy for speed), and the reflective, rational center of our brains (which is more accurate, but not quite as fast). The 4Rs give us better access to our rational, thinking brains. But they do more than that: The 4Rs greatly improve the quality of the data upon which we make those thoughtful decisions. Although they won't make past mistakes disappear, nor prevent us from ever making a mistake again, the 4Rs ensure that we are making financial decisions in accordance with the two rules of financial intelligence. That is, the 4Rs allow us to make decisions aligned with our most important personal values, and they encourage us to take financial actions that prepare us for the certainty of uncertainty.

As you'll see in the next four chapters, the 4Rs are a structured, step-by-step process. When practiced regularly, the 4Rs create a strong foundation for making smart, responsible, values-based decisions about money (or anything else in life).

PRACTICE, PRACTICE, PRACTICE

In Chapter 1, you saw how your brain is wired so that emotions and habits take precedence over logic when it comes to highly charged events. In this chapter, you saw how the 4Rs can help you avoid making costly financial mistakes. Using the 4Rs can rewire your brain to respond reflectively vs. reacting reflexively based only on emotions. The 4Rs—Recognize, Reflect, Reframe, and Respond—are deceptively simple. When people first learn about them, they often think, "What's the big deal? Is this all I have to do to make good financial decisions?" You may be skeptical that a process that seems so uncomplicated can transform your financial life. But, here's the catch: The 4Rs don't come easily to us—at least not at first. To be effective, you must practice the 4Rs regularly, preferably multiple times every day. The 4Rs become new habits that you need to deliberately add to your daily routines. That regular practice is key to changing your brain's approach to problem-solving and decision-making. Dianne Laughton, an Iowa-based financial adviser, is an enthusiastic 4Rs user.

> When I first started doing the "Freeze Game"—stopping to recognize everything I was experiencing—it was a very methodical process. I wrote everything down in a notebook, starting with, "What am I feeling right now?" Then I reflected on my values, making more notes. Asking, "What do I want to change?" then writing that down too. It was a little tedious and took some time, especially since I had committed to do it at least several times a day. But that practice paid off. I felt it did take time initially for it to become more automatic. I now tell people that you can do the 4Rs in a millisecond. Recently, I had an older client who called me and wanted to meet. As soon as I picked up the phone, I recognized that I had a momentary flash of irritation. Then I realized, "It's not her, it's the awful stock market." When we did meet, I was able to help her recognize her understandable fears, reflect on her goals, and ultimately support her in staying with the long-term financial plan she had set.[6]

As Dianne discovered, changing habits requires commitment and persistence. Think about the last time you tried to change your behavior. Maybe you decided to lose a few pounds, or become more physically active. In each case, the process is simple: maybe it's a matter of eating less, or eating more fruits and vegetables, or signing up for a yoga class, or getting up an hour earlier each day to take a walk. Maybe it's a decision to quit smoking. None of the things we need to do to make positive changes are complicated. But they can be hard to do. For example, nothing could be simpler—or harder—than not lighting up a cigarette. Why? Because our brains are wired to keep doing what we've already been doing. Similarly, the 4Rs are both simple and hard. They are not complicated, but it will take some effort to make them part of how you live and think. You will need to decide that you don't want to be at the mercy of your reflexive brain. You will need to decide that your financial well-being is worth the initial discomfort of developing new habits. You will need to decide that you want to be someone who makes good financial decisions that benefit you, your family, and your community.

In the next four chapters you'll learn what you need to know and do to become an expert in the four essential skills of financial intelligence.

ENDNOTES

1. Neuroscientist Jeffrey Schwartz, author of *The Mind and the Brain: Neuroplasticity and the Power of Mental Force*, published in 2003 by Harper Perennial, has reviewed and confirmed the ability of the 4R model to disrupt habitual responses to highly charged events. He and I, with co-author Pablo Gaito, have written "That's Not The Way We Do Things Around Here," which integrates my 4R approach with Schwartz's similar approach, applied in this case to human behavioral change in organizations. *strategy+business*. Booz & Company (forthcoming).
2. Goleman, Daniel, 2000. *Working with Emotional Intelligence*. Bantam Books. 74–75.
3. Rock, David, and Jeffrey Schwartz. May 2006. *The Neuroscience of Leadership*. Strategy+Business: www.strategy-business.com/article/06207?pg=1 :2.
4. Schwartz, Jeffrey. 2003. *The Mind and the Brain: Neuroplasticity and the Power of Mental Force*. Harper Perennial. 234.
5. Ongoing personal communications between Jeffrey Schwartz and Doug Lennick, 2008–2009.
6. Interview, September 2008.

5 | *Recognizing*

To manage the emotions that affect your financial decisions, you must first *recognize* them. That's easier said than done. Most of us think we're pretty self-aware. By the time we get to be adults, we think we know ourselves pretty well. And most of us like to think that we're being objective, even when we're not. But as we learned from Chapter 1, when it comes to money, we're simply not aware of how our physiological state is clouding our thinking. So the first step to greater financial intelligence is to recognize exactly what you are really thinking, feeling, and doing when in the throes of a stimulating financial situation. And to be able to recognize your cognitive, emotional, and physical states when you really need to, you must train yourself in advance. You want to become so skilled at recognition that it becomes second nature for you. By practicing the skill of recognition you will transform yourself from a *reflexive responder* to a *reflective recognizer.*

RECOGNITION IN THE MOMENT: THE EXPERIENTIAL TRIANGLE

At any given moment, there is a phenomenal amount of activity going on within us—much of it we're not even aware of. Each day, the average person:

- Thinks 12,000 thoughts
- Pumps 2,000 gallons of blood through 60,000 miles of blood vessels
- Blinks his or her eyes 17,000 times
- Breathes 23,040 times
- Sheds 14 million particles of skin
- Replaces 400 billion cells

All of our life experiences fall into one of three categories:

- Cognitive (our thoughts)
- Emotional (our feelings)
- Physical (our physiology and our actions)

Think of these three categories of experience as points on a triangle. Thoughts, feelings, and actions are interconnected and usually

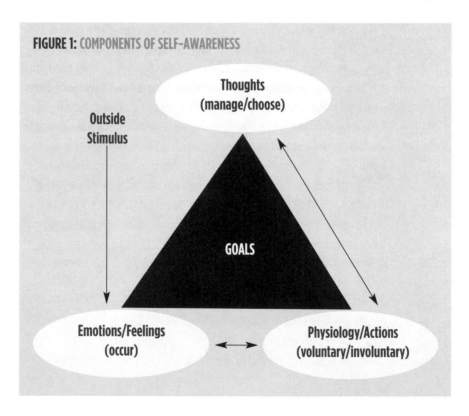

FIGURE 1: COMPONENTS OF SELF-AWARENESS

influence one another. For example, if I *think* about someone who punched me yesterday, I am likely to *feel* angry; my heart rate will go up (*physiology*) and I may clench my fists (*action*) at the thought of what happened. My feelings and actions may even set off a new cycle of the experiential triangle, perhaps causing me to think about exacting revenge, which in turn stimulates new feelings, and so on.

Try this to experience the powerful connections between thoughts, emotions, and physical responses.[1]

- First, close your eyes and concentrate for two minutes on a memory of something that happened that really made you angry.
- Focus your attention on what happened and who was involved, and think about that situation for two minutes.
- After two minutes, open your eyes and recognize what you just experienced relative to your thoughts, your emotions, and your physical being.

What you will notice, if you are self-aware, is that you thought about what made you angry. It usually was a person, and within two minutes you might have thought about how that person angered you more than one time, or about other times that person angered you.

You may also have noticed that your emotional state changed. You might have become angry again, or you might have felt guilt or regret. Your focus on your initial response may change how you are feeling emotionally, within the two minutes. You probably also noticed that you were beginning to feel physical tension in your shoulders, your heart rate picking up, and your breathing becoming shallower.

Everything that happened to you was a result of what you were thinking about. As my colleague neuroscientist Jeff Schwartz points out, "Focus is power. What you choose to focus your attention on has power over your emotional and physical state."[2]

Now, take the exercise to another step:

- Take a few deep breaths, close your eyes, and for the next two minutes, imagine that your brain is a radio receiver and that you have three channels permanently programmed into your automatic selections. One channel is the gratitude channel. The second channel is the love channel. The third channel is the beauty channel. For the next two minutes, turn on one of those channels. Depending on the channel you choose, focus completely on what you are grateful for, or whom you love deeply, or what beautiful aspects of life and your environment you most appreciate (for instance, mountains, ocean, desert, etc.).

- Now, open your eyes and recognize what you have experienced.

If you're like most people, you will notice that your emotional state became much more peaceful. You began to feel love, began to feel relaxed, and began to feel calm. You might have thought about all the things you are grateful for; or you may have discovered that you have a deep appreciation for certain people or natural settings. What you will surely notice is that your physiological state has changed. Your heart rate and breathing are slower, and your face is relaxed. You might have even noticed a smile come across your face. Once again you have discovered the power of focus, and the surprising amount of control you have over what you think and feel.

These exercises help us understand the importance and power of recognizing our experiential triangle. Managing our thoughts, emotions, and physical state is central to our ability to make smart, responsible, values-based financial decisions. Therefore, cultivating the art of recognizing our thoughts, feelings, and emotions is a crucial skill of financial intelligence. Recognition skills help us fully access our experiences so that we have information we need to *choose* our responses to events, rather than automatically (and often unconsciously) *reacting* to them.

FREEZE!

One of the simplest and most powerful ways to cultivate the skill of recognition is to practice the Freeze Game.[3] When you use the Freeze Game, you declare a short time-out from whatever you happen to be doing in the moment. Imagine you've just hit the pause button on the DVD of your life. Then ask yourself these three questions:

1. **What am I thinking right now?**
   For example, what am I saying to myself inside my head? Am I thinking about a problem at work? A relationship issue? The weather?
2. **What am I feeling emotionally?**
   Emotions are words, not sentences; for example, I feel sad, excited, angry, frustrated.
3. **What am I doing and what is happening with me physically, right now?**
   For example, am I sitting or standing? Am I smiling or frowning? What's the look on my face? Is my heart racing or calm? Is my breathing pattern normal or accelerated? Am I tense or relaxed?

As you've probably noticed, each question is intended to help you become aware of one aspect of your experiential triangle of thoughts, feelings, and actions/physiological state. Why not try playing the Freeze Game right now? You can jot down your answers in the box on the next page.

When you played the Freeze Game, what did you become aware of that you hadn't noticed before? Many people are surprised by how much is going on internally and externally, even when engaged in a supposedly simple activity such as reading this book. While writing this, I just paused to play the Freeze Game and here is what I noticed:

- **Thoughts:** I hope to get this chapter finished this week, and I'm remembering I also have a lot of other things to do this week.
- **Feelings:** Impatient, excited, optimistic.
- **Actions:** Physically, I'm noticing that my hands are cold and my stomach is growling; also that I've been tapping my feet under the desk without realizing it before, and that my brow is furrowed.

My experiential triangle at the moment is not too dramatic, and probably yours was not either. But imagine now your experiential triangle when faced with a stimulating situation related to your finances. Imagine this common response to some disturbing financial triggers:

EXERCISE: PLAY THE FREEZE GAME

What am I thinking right now?_____

What am I feeling emotionally?

☐ Angry   ☐ Helpful   ☐ Frustrated   ☐ Playful   ☐ Tired
☐ Happy   ☐ Sad   ☐ Confident   ☐ Scared   ☐ Excited
☐ _____   ☐ _____   ☐ _____

What am I doing and what is happening with me physically right now?

☐ Breathing   ☐ Heart Rate   ☐ Muscles   ☐ Jaw
☐ Movements   ☐ Appetite

You've just read a headline that unemployment has just exceeded 10 percent, and that the worst is yet to come. Your heart rate picks up. You begin to read the article about how high unemployment may lead us back into the recession. So you think to yourself, "I'd better move all of my money to a safe instrument. I've been hearing that the one category that seems to have been rising and will continue to rise is gold. Gold is selling at $1,200 per ounce and some say it may pass $2,000, so I'm going to get out of the investments I'm in and move almost all my investment money into gold, hoping this will protect me from what undoubtedly will be a prolonged recession."

Later that day, you open the latest monthly statement of your retirement account. Even before you tear the envelope open, your heart rate is rising (which you may not notice). You see that your portfolio has lost $50,000 in the last three months, and your heart rate and respiration increase again (which you may still not notice). You think to yourself, "This is not acceptable. I've got to move what money I have left out of stock funds and into something safer." You're feeling panicky (which you may not notice). You dial the number of your 401(k) company with the intention of selling your stock funds and plunking the proceeds into some CDs. Hold on! You've made a decision that doesn't make sense unless you need to draw on your retirement funds in the near future. You've made a decision based on false logic, "I must eliminate risk from my current retirement portfolio," and unexamined emotions (fear and panic). The only way to keep yourself from making a bad decision is to train your brain to respond differently to those emotions. And the first step is to *recognize* them.

Now imagine what would have happened in this hypothetical scenario if you had played the Freeze Game. It would be ideal to play the Freeze Game as soon as you saw the headline. If you had, you likely would have recognized that your emotional state was clouding your judgment. That doesn't mean it's necessarily wrong to put money into gold. It does mean that a reflexive response to divest everything and go to gold would violate one of the rules of financial intelligence: Prepare yourself for the certainty of uncertainty. In this case, your thoughts are suggesting there is a certainty about the future, which deeper logic would help you realize cannot be true. Not that we won't have another recession, but we can't be certain that we will. Not that gold won't go up, but we can't be certain that it will. Moving all my money into one investment portfolio and into a certain instrument assumes I am able to determine what is going to happen. Using the Freeze Game allows us to catch these flaws in our thinking before they can cause us financial harm.

PRACTICING RECOGNITION IN THE MOMENT

The example above should give you a sense of the contribution of recognition to financial intelligence. Recognition *is* a powerful tool, but only if you use it. If you're not accustomed to taking time out for recognition, it probably won't occur to you to hit the pause button when you're in the throes of an emotionally charged situation. Your ability to call on recognition when you really need it—such as during a highly stimulating financial situation—depends on your ability to make recognition second nature. That takes practice. And that means playing the Freeze Game dozens of times a day for at least three weeks (research shows that's the minimum length of time needed to establish a consistent habit). The more you play the Freeze Game, the more natural it will become to check in with yourself to see what you're thinking and feeling and doing. Once the Freeze Game is a habit, you are that much more likely to use it when the financial stakes are high. As you regularly play the Freeze Game, you'll probably begin to notice many other benefits in your life. You'll develop more self-awareness, and that deeper understanding of how you really think, feel, and act may translate into more positive relationships with family and friends, and even more productive behavior at work. Of course, simply recognizing your experiential triangle during many life moments won't in and of itself make you a different person. But knowledge is power and self-knowledge is even more powerful. As you begin to recognize how you show up moment-to-moment, you have the opportunity to decide whether you're happy with your experience or you'd like to change it in a more positive direction.

RECOGNIZING THINKING PATTERNS

Our supposedly rational thought processes may not be as objective as we think. That's why it's useful to pay attention to the ways in which patterns of thought affect our actions. Our ability to make smart, responsible, values-based decisions is very much dependent on the way we *typically* think. One aspect of our thinking patterns is especially important to financial decision-making: mental biases. Mental biases are a form of "self-spin" that fool us into thinking we are being logical and objective when we really aren't.

RECOGNIZING MENTAL BIASES

Everyone has mental biases. And they're not necessarily bad. They are shorthand principles that the brain uses to manage the thousands of decisions and actions we must take in any given day. For instance, we may have a mental bias that "people are trustworthy." This principle allows us to deal with people in an efficient way. By assuming that most people can be trusted, we feel fine about answering the door, asking for directions, working on a project with a fellow employee, eating food prepared by others, and going to sleep at night next to our spouse. Imagine what your life would be like if every time you came into contact with another person, you had to figure out whether or not that person could be trusted. Your daily life would probably collapse under the strain of gauging each person's trustworthiness from scratch. So, for the most part, our mental bias that "people are trustworthy" is highly functional—even though it's not completely true. In fact some people are not trustworthy. Some people could harm us, and everyone has had occasional negative experiences with untrustworthy people. Mental biases become a problem only when we forget that we have them. For example, assuming that people are trustworthy can blind us to the warning signs that a particular person may not have our best interests at heart. That's why we need to *recognize* our mental biases, not so we can eliminate them (an impossible task), but so we can be aware of how they could influence the financial decisions we make.

When it comes to financial decisions, mental biases operate in various ways; for example, they can cause us to ignore important data, attach too much importance to certain data, or encourage us to make decisions based on misguided beliefs about ourselves or the situation we're in. When in the throes of a mental bias, we think we're making an analytical decision when we're really not.

Several researchers have conducted brain research that demonstrates the degree to which mental biases disrupt our ability to think analytically. One study was carried out shortly before the 2004 United States presidential election. Thirty men, half of whom described themselves as strong Republicans and half as strong Democrats, were asked to evaluate contradictory statements that had been made by both Republican and Democratic presidential nominees while undergoing a functional magnetic resonance imaging (fMRI) scan. The brain scans showed that the part of the brain associated with reasoning (the dorsolateral prefrontal cortex) was not involved when assessing the statements. That means that when people with partisan biases were asked to consider their candidates' inconsistent statements, their brains' logic centers never came into play! But the part of the brain involved in processing emotion (the orbitofrontal cortex) was working overtime.[4]

HEALTHY FOOD FRANCHISE: LESSONS IN MENTAL BIASES

A number of years ago, I invested in a franchised restaurant business that offered a healthy fast food alternative to some of the less healthy choices available in the marketplace. This investment was certainly consistent with the health value that my wife and I share. However, not all of my other values, especially wisdom, were getting enough focus and attention. As the years went by, the company continued to require new capital. I repeatedly invested good money after bad. Why? Because I focused only on data that confirmed my optimism. I was told by people operating the business that things would get better because the concept was working in other markets and existing customers were loyal. I chose to accept that because I tend to be optimistic and confident. I had a very strong bias against losing money. I ignored or explained away data and advice that did not support my emotional belief in the business. My accountant, my attorney, and even another investor and member of our board who had more experience in the restaurant business than I did all said it didn't look good given our expense structure. Serious restructuring needed to take place and even with that, it was highly unlikely our investment would ever pay off.

Because I did not accept information about the dangers of investing more in the business, I moved from being confident and optimistic to being overconfident and excessively optimistic. The dopamine raging through me had turned off my risk assessment system. The investors, of which my wife and I were the largest, lost. Once I made the investment, there was no way to exit when I should have without losing my initial investment, a substantial sum. But my lack of judgment and my aversion to losing that initial investment caused us to lose three times more money than we would have lost had I been able to exercise better judgment. Fortunately, my wife and I had not put all our eggs in that one basket, so we were able to weather a significant, but ultimately unnecessary, loss. What's more, our investment in the restaurant franchise had an "opportunity cost" beyond our financial loss: Had we moved out of that investment sooner, I could have directed money and attention to a business that was both consistent with my family's values and had a better chance of success.

That experience helped inspire the creation of the 4Rs. I knew that I was not the only person who had experienced a failure in judgment. And if I, with all my financial expertise, was capable of making a big financial mistake, then anyone could. I learned an expensive lesson, but I could "afford it" in the absolute sense. However, being stupid with my money isn't what I had in mind. What about the majority of people who did not have the financial safety net that I had created for my family? What about the majority of people for whom financial misjudgments could be devastating?

MANAGING MENTAL BIASES

We've already seen how hard it can be to make decisions based on logic rather than emotion. So it's essential that our logic is based on good data. Mental biases are patterns of thinking that distort our ability to evaluate situations objectively.

To better understand how mental biases can derail sound financial judgment, let's look in more detail at my experience with the restaurant franchise. I'm an optimist. I see the silver lining in most situations, and that positive attitude keeps me motivated to work on a solution to any challenge. Though my optimism is a strength, too much of any strength can turn into a weakness. So, in the case of the restaurant franchise, my optimism became over-optimism. It drowned out information that conflicted with my optimistic view. My confidence that I could do what was needed to make the business successful morphed into overconfidence that I could succeed despite market conditions that made success very unlikely.

COMMON MENTAL BIASES

To guard against mental biases, we must first learn to recognize them. Try to spot these common biases in your own thinking:

Overconfidence. While confidence is an asset when it comes to financial decision-making, overconfidence, that is excessive confidence, can cause us to overestimate our abilities, as I did while an investor in the restaurant franchise. Confidence helps us accurately assess our abilities and the risks inherent in a particular financial decision. Research demonstrates that people who are appropriately confident achieve the most in their personal and professional lives.

Take, for example, a famous experiment conducted by the legendary Harvard psychologist David McClelland. People were asked to toss rings over a peg from any distance they chose. Some chose to throw their rings at a very short distance from the peg, therefore assuring that they would succeed. Others tossed their rings from such a long distance that it would be a fluke if they were able to succeed. But achievement-oriented individuals studied the task carefully and chose a distance from the peg that was not too close and not too far away. They chose a distance from the peg where they had a reasonable, but not certain, chance of successfully tossing the ring over the peg. We might think of those people who tossed their ring from very close to the peg as lacking in confidence, while the people who chose an extremely far distance from the ring as being overconfident. The truly confident individuals studied the landscape, made a calculated assessment of risk, and set their distance accordingly. And they succeeded most—but not all—of the time. So overconfidence is that tendency to think we can get that ring over that peg even when the peg is too far away. Often we are overconfident because we have a tendency to view ourselves as better than average. But if you mistake luck for talent, before too long, you will make bad decisions. And some of those decisions can be very destructive to you and your family.

Excessive Optimism. Closely related to overconfidence, this is the bias that can cause us to overestimate how frequently we will experience favorable outcomes and underestimate how often we will experience less than desirable results. Psychologists David Armor and Shelley Taylor reviewed a number of studies that demonstrated the prevalence of over-optimism in a wide range of judgments. For example, almost all newlyweds in the United States expect that their marriages will last their whole lifetimes, despite their awareness of current divorce rate statistics.[5] This bias can be hard to manage, because while excessive optimism can taint a decision, a measure of optimism is important. To a couple of newlyweds, optimism is critical to developing a strong and resilient marriage. To financial decision-makers, optimism can be essential to achieving positive financial outcomes. For instance, Fred Mandell, who left a lucrative job as a corporate executive to become a full-time sculptor, said that his optimism about the future helped him move forward despite the financial risk he was taking. But for many others, it's easy for optimism to morph into over-optimism, and when we do, it is very difficult for us to see the real facts of a situation clearly.

Confirmation Bias. This is a tendency to look for or interpret information in a way that confirms what we already think. Confirmation bias also involves ignoring information that would contradict what we already think. Financial adviser Dianne Laughton and her husband live in rural Le Mars, Iowa, not far from Sioux City. She recalls a time when they lost a fair amount of money in a commodities trading scheme. They bought the sales pitch of a commodities broker who painted a very exciting picture of how much money they could make within commodities trading "clubs," in which groups of investors would pool their money and presumably spread out the risk. Dianne is, by training and temperament, careful and financially savvy. She believed that they were making an objective decision to invest, but her logic was clouded by confirmation bias. She had some relatives who had successfully traded in commodities, while some of her neighbors were farmers who ended up losing their farms because of commodities trading losses. Dianne and her husband knew there were risks, but they chose to pay more attention to the example of people who succeeded in commodities trading than those who suffered losses. Thanks to Dianne's financial savvy, she didn't overinvest in those investments, so the financial loss, while painful, was offset by gains from other, wiser investments.

Availability Bias. This is the tendency to place too much weight on information that is readily available or easy to understand, instead of paying attention to information that is less available or more difficult to understand. Back in the late 1980s, Fred Mandell, the former financial services executive turned sculptor mentioned earlier, became a limited partner in a venture to convert large Victorian houses into condominiums. Before he decided to make the investment, Fred did his homework. He visited the properties. He reviewed the business plan prepared by the two general partners. One of the general partners was a friend, whom Fred knew had made successful real estate investments in the past. Based on all this information, Fred felt comfortable about making the investment. But the venture failed. Fred lost a lot of money. Part of the reason the project failed was that the real estate market took a downturn, reducing the profit potential. But the major culprit was the mismanagement and misuse of funds by the general partner Fred didn't know. Fred had never thought to investigate the second general partner's background and track record because he trusted his friend's recommendation. The need for that information was not so obvious to Fred. And independent information about the second partner's background would have been somewhat more difficult to access. Fred did his homework—but relied on data that the general partners had presented him, the easily available kind.

Familiarity Bias. This is a tendency to apply too much weight to financial options with which we have had prior contact. Suppose, for example, you want to open a savings account. A logical step would be to do some research about which banks offer the highest interest rates. Many of us, however, simply take our money to our neighborhood bank, because it's familiar to us, without assessing whether it will give us the best results. Our bias toward the familiar can affect a broad array of financial decisions, such as choosing a financial adviser or mutual fund company based on prior contact.

Erin and Doug Livermore, a young couple, put their Syracuse, New York, home on the market when Doug, an army captain, was reassigned to a base in Georgia. To help them sell the house, they chose the real estate agent who had sold them the house a number of years earlier. Because they already knew the agent, they didn't think they needed to look for anyone else, nor did they ask hard questions about their agent's plan to sell their house in a sluggish housing market. What they didn't know—because they never asked—was that their agent was coping with the housing slump by taking on another full-time job, leaving the agent with little time or energy to creatively market their home. As a result, their house languished on the market for many months, while they watched their savings drain away paying the mortgage as well as housing costs at their new location.

All these biases are natural—our brains are wired to encourage them. So don't beat yourself up if you've let them trip you up in the past. The important thing now is to learn to spot them when they creep into your thoughts, and recognize how they could interfere with your ability to make smart, responsible, values-based financial decisions.

Use your responses to the Mental Biases Exercise to begin to recognize how mental biases play into your financial decisions. For the next few weeks, make a point of using the worksheet on the next two pages as you consider any decision. This will give you practice in recognizing your thinking patterns. The more skilled you are in recognizing mental biases, the easier it will be for you to recognize them in action when you are faced with a highly charged financial situation.

RECOGNIZING EMOTIONAL PATTERNS

One of my personal recognition moments was realizing how excited I got about an opportunity a few years ago to make a substantial amount of money investing in a rock quarry. Despite my optimism about the opportunity, the operational realities of getting the rock out of the ground and into the market did not materialize in a productive way, and soon the business went into bankruptcy. As I write this book, I am quite confident that I will lose most or all of my investment. The difference between this deal and others I've been involved in before is that this time I recognized my excitement. I used recognition (and all the 4Rs) to limit the scale of a speculative investment to an amount that would not negatively affect my financial well-being. To fund the rock quarry investment, I took money

RECOGNIZING MENTAL BIASES WORKSHEET

Briefly describe a financial decision in which, looking back, you were not completely satisfied with the results.

Overconfidence

Did I overestimate my knowledge or skills in dealing with this situation?
Did this particular bias have an effect on my ultimate decision?
If yes, jot down some thoughts about how this mental bias influenced you.

Excessive Optimism

Did I overestimate the likelihood of a positive outcome in this situation?
Did this particular bias have an effect on my ultimate decision?
If yes, jot down some thoughts about how this mental bias influenced you.

RECOGNIZING MENTAL BIASES WORKSHEET *(CONTINUED)*

Confirmation Bias

Did I unconsciously seek out information that would justify a decision I emotionally wanted to make?
Did I ignore information that might have led me to make a different decision?
Did this particular bias have an effect on my ultimate decision?
If yes, jot down some thoughts about how this mental bias influenced you.

Availability Bias

Did I focus on information that was readily available or easy to understand?
Did I fail to seek out relevant information that was harder to find or might be more difficult to understand?
Did this particular bias have an effect on my ultimate decision?
If yes, jot down some thoughts about how this mental bias influenced you.

Familiarity Bias

Did I make a financial decision based on what was familiar to me, or would be most convenient to carry out?
Did this particular bias have an effect on my ultimate decision?
If yes, jot down some thoughts about how this mental bias influenced you.

out of the stock market when it was at historic highs. In effect, I was investing profits from other investments into this investment, so it was a smart place to get money for a risky investment. What's more, I didn't let excessive optimism or overconfidence blur my assessment of the investment. I knew it was speculative. I knew there was a chance I could lose all that I had invested. I used recognition of my mental biases to keep me from investing more money that I was willing to lose.

I also recognized that in the past, when reacting to an equally exciting opportunity, I overinvested. This time I used recognition of my tendency toward excessive confidence to remind myself that this project might not work. I have been asked multiple times to make additional investments into the rock quarry project. Although in the past I probably would have done so, in this case I have not. This time I recognize that the investment will either pay off or not. If the rock quarry investment does pay off, great. I'll have made enough from my initial investment. If the rock quarry investment fails, I will have lost enough money from my initial investment, and I'll be glad I didn't invest more. Thus, recognizing my thoughts and emotions has allowed me to enjoy pursuing certain exciting financial opportunities, without negatively affecting my overall financial responsibilities and goals.

RECOGNIZING PATTERNS

When you play the Freeze Game frequently and consistently you may begin to notice similarities in how you react to everyday situations, positive and negative, at home and work. You may begin to see a pattern in your responses to situations as varied as being cut off by an aggressive driver, dealing with a difficult co-worker, tucking your kids in for the night, or facing a huge mound of laundry. Recognition of these patterns can further increase your self-awareness about common reactions that can trip you up in your decision-making and behavior. We know that the emotions that cloud our financial judgment are those that are strongly positive or negative. So we can increase our recognition of emotional patterns by looking at past experiences that have prompted us to respond with strong emotions. You may, for instance, want to ask yourself the recognition questions this way: "During what experiences in my past have I felt happy, excited, hopeful, angry, sad, or fearful?" Answering such questions can help you recognize some of your most important emotional patterns. Try the Recognizing Emotional Patterns Exercise on the next page to gain a deeper understanding of how you frequently respond to significant life events.

As you look at your descriptions of emotionally charged situations in the exercise, what emotional patterns do you see? Does watching your kids play sports bring out the best in you or the worst in you? For example, are you happiest when you're watching your kids play sports, or does watching your kids play sports make you feel angry with coaches, officials, or even your own child? And what behavioral patterns do you see that are associated with certain emotionally charged situations? Do you find yourself smiling and cheering on your children, or do you find yourself yelling at your child or the coaches?

WHAT TO ASK FAMILY AND FRIENDS

Recalling situations that trigger strong emotions is a good way to build your recognition skill. But all of us have blind spots that keep us from noticing some of our patterns, or prevent us from realizing their full effect. To flesh out your understanding of emotional patterns, it's a good idea to also get feedback from the people closest to you, say your spouse, children, friends, or colleagues at work. Use the Feedback About My Patterns Worksheet to organize your request for feedback and to record their responses.

When you ask for feedback, be prepared to hear some things that may not be flattering. Don't use this as an opportunity to try to "explain away" or defend any behavior. If you act defensively, you will dry up your source of information when you need it in the future. But do ask for any more information that would help you understand your patterns and the effect they may have, positively or negatively, on others. Most of all, express appreciation for the person's feedback and enlist that person's help in recognizing future

EXERCISE: RECOGNIZING EMOTIONAL PATTERNS

Emotions	Situations	Related Actions	Related Thoughts
	List 1–3 situations, preferably situations that reoccur.	What do you do, either voluntarily or involuntarily, when you are in this situation?	What attitudes or ideas do you have about this situation when you are experiencing it?
I am **happiest** when			
I am very **excited** when			
I feel **hopeful** when			
I feel **angry** when			
I feel **sad** when			
I feel **fearful** when			

instances of negative patterns. You might want to end the feedback discussion by saying: "In the future, will you let me know if you think I'm reacting too intensely about a situation, for instance, if I seem 'irrationally exuberant' or negative about a situation? And if you see me improving my reactions, I would also welcome you commenting on that."

—◦◦◦—

As you've seen, the mere act of recognizing your thoughts, emotions, and physical state can go a long way to preventing emotionally driven responses to significant financial situations. But recognizing is only the first of four powerful financial intelligence skills. In the next

FEEDBACK ABOUT MY PATTERNS WORKSHEET		
Emotional Reaction	**Typical Situation** When does this emotional reaction happen?	**Related Actions** What do I do or say (and how) when in this situation?
What emotional reactions do I have that annoy you or worry you the most?		
What emotional reactions do I have that you enjoy the most?		

chapter, you'll have a chance to reap more of the benefits of the 4Rs, by using *reflecting* to put the rational center of your brain back in control of your financial decision-making process.

ENDNOTE

1. I was taught this exercise by Fred Luskin (author of *Forgive for Good* and director of the Forgiveness Project at Stanford University) and performance psychologist Rick Aberman, Ph.D, my partner at the Lennick Aberman Group.
2. Personal conversation with author. Concept also presented in Rock, David, and Jeffrey Schwartz. May 2006. *The Neuroscience of Leadership.* Strategy+Business: www.strategy-business.com/article/06207?pg=1.
3. The Freeze Game was introduced to me by psychologist Rick Aberman, Ph.D., a founding partner of the Lennick Aberman Group.
4. Westen, Drew, *et al.* 2006. "The Neural Bases of Motivated Reasoning: An fMRI Study of Emotional Constraints on Political Judgment During the U.S. Presidential Election of 2004." *Journal of Cognitive Neuroscience*: www.mitpressjournals.org/doi/abs/10.1162/jocn.2006.18.11.1947?cookieSet=1&journalCode=jocn.
5. Armor, David A., and Shelley E. Taylor. "When Predictions Fail: The Dilemma of Unrealistic Optimism." In Gilovich, Thomas. 2002. *Heuristics and Biases: The Psychology of Intuitive Judgment.* Cambridge, UK: Cambridge University Press.

6 | *Reflecting*

I live in Minnesota, which is famous for its long, cold, and snowy winters. I'm not complaining: I take advantage of the weather to stay fit. I shovel snow to promote my physical fitness. And while I'm clearing the driveway, I practice *reflecting* to maintain my decision-making fitness. Neighbors who pass by have no idea that the guy muttering to himself while heaving piles of snow is actually reflecting on his most important values. I begin with my first value: *Family*. In my mind I call up pictures of my mom and dad, my wife, my kids, my daughter-in-law, and my grandson. I also envision my mom, who passed away years ago, and my dad who passed away during the writing of this book. Both are still present for me. As I picture my family, I reflect on how grateful I am for them, how happy they make me, and how much I want to make them happy. Next, I reflect on another value: *Happiness*. I say to myself, "Be happy." Of course, I'm already happy because I've been thinking about my family. Then I move to my third value: *Wisdom*. I say to myself, "Seek wisdom." I think about how it's less important to know a lot than it is to be wise. And I believe in the pursuit of wisdom because I want my life to have meaning. The driveway is half clear now as I turn to my fourth value:

Integrity. I say to myself, "Behave with integrity." I remind myself to tell the truth, keep my promises, stand up for what is right, and act in alignment with all my other values. Then I move to my fifth value: *Service*. I say to myself, "Be of service to someone else today." I think of what I can do today to live out that value. I remind myself to put some money in the Salvation Army bucket when I get to the office later this morning. And finally, I think about my sixth value: *Health*. I say to myself, "Make healthy choices." I make a note to take my vitamins and have some fruit when I get back inside. By now, the driveway is all clear. And maybe more importantly, I've connected my most important values in a way that sets the stage for everything I will do that day.

If it's not snowing, I still get outside and work with our plants. I'll also reflect on my values in the shower. One way or another, before I leave the house, I've gone through all my values. It sets the tone for my day. In effect, I make an appointment with my values. I have lots of things on my daily schedule, but no matter what I'm doing, I want my activities to be infused with those values. Reflecting on my values also has a benefit very specific to financial decision-making: Rehearsing those values rewires my neural circuits and contributes to improving my emotional and cognitive response patterns. When a challenging situation comes up, financially or otherwise, I want to be able to find my values in the dark. I want to be able to access them automatically whenever I face a financial decision. I want my internal values to be what stimulates me, rather than the external events that may either excite or frighten me. Reflecting on my values doesn't guarantee that I'll never make a stupid financial decision, but it does increase the likelihood that I'll make decisions that are aligned with values rather than driven by emotions. And that's why I reflect on my values a number of times during the day. On an elevator. Walking a few blocks to a lunch meeting. Driving home from work. On the way to the mailbox.

PRACTICING REFLECTION

In the last chapter, you had a chance to hone your recognition skill. The recognition exercises were intended to increase your awareness of what you are experiencing in a particular moment and of your habitual responses to highly charged emotional events. Armed with that crucial information, you are in a much better position to practice reflection.

The primary purpose of reflection is to change the source of stimulation from the outside in to the inside out. Reflection begins the process of creating an internal source of stimulation, one based on your moral principles, personal values, and the big picture of your life—including an accurate understanding of your current finances. In this chapter, you will learn three types of reflection, all of which enhance your financial intelligence:

- **Preparing to be reflective.** Like any habit, reflection often requires a "cueing mechanism" to help us get into the frame of mind required for reflective thought. In this chapter, you'll have a chance to experiment with activities that get you into the right frame of mind for reflection.
- **Making reflection a daily habit.** As with recognition, your ability to use reflection when you need it most requires routine practice. This means making reflection a habit, taking time to be reflective several times a day.
- **Using your reflection skill in the moments** when you are being actively stimulated by a financial situation.

PREPARING YOUR MIND FOR REFLECTION

Many of us live in a state of chronic physiological stress. Juggling the demands of family, work, and community obligations can leave us in a chronic physiological state in which our danger system is always operating at some level. It's hard to be thoughtful when you are preoccupied, distracted, stressed, excited, or fearful. That's why it's necessary to do something to help us break from our routines or detach from the emotions of the moment. Of course, practicing recognition is key to clearing the path to reflective thought. We stop action and observe what is going on in us. Stopping to take note of your thoughts, feelings, and state of being can interrupt any stress or excessive busyness that can make it difficult to reflect. In addition to practicing recognition, there are a number of practices that calm the mind and body, paving the way for a more reflective and rational state of mind.

Reflection can be enhanced by a whole variety of preparatory activities. Dr. Herbert Benson, founding president of the Mind/Body Medical Institute, calls these activities "triggers" because they change our physiology in ways that in turn trigger well-being and improved performance. Triggering activities include prayer or meditation, listening to your favorite music, biking or walking in nature, soaking in a hot tub, or even mundane tasks like yard work or dishes.

One of the most powerful triggers for reflection is deep breathing. When our danger system is on, our breathing is shallow. We are breathing deeply enough to stay alive, but not deeply enough to feel good—or think and act at our best. Taking time out to breathe deeply and slowly will change our whole physiology in a matter of moments. We feel less harried, more relaxed, and better able to deal with whatever challenge we may be facing. I learned a deep breathing technique many years ago (see the Mindful Breathing Exercise), and it has helped me deal with countless demanding situations. For instance, I was testifying at a regulatory body in Washington, D.C., not long after September 11, 2001. Everything about the experience was unpleasant. The hearing was held in a federal building where I was escorted to a cramped and sterile hearing room. On one side of the table sat the three panel members leading the day-long inquiry. I sat opposite the regulators, with my lawyers on one side of me and the stenographer on my right. The regulators were clearly asking questions in a way designed to push my buttons. I felt the stress coming. I recognized that I was going to have a bad moment. I understood the emotions I was having, that I hated being there. I felt the rush of warmth that accompanied my anger and frustration. My heart rate was picking up. Then there was an unexpected break in the inquiry caused by a problem with the stenographer's equipment.

My lawyers wanted to use the time to strategize about my subsequent responses. I told them, "No. I need to think by myself." I looked over the heads of the panel, focusing my vision on the opposite wall. I took some slow, deep breaths. Then I turned on the "love channel." I pictured my wife and my children, my mom and dad, my grandparents, and even all my dogs, alive and deceased. As I went through this process, I began to notice my face was relaxing. When I felt a smile coming across my face, I knew I was ready to testify. Breathing and the love channel saved the day for me.

EXERCISE: MINDFUL BREATHING

You can practice mindful breathing practically anywhere, and even a minute or two of mindful breathing will help you feel clearer and calmer. To get the greatest benefits from mindful breathing, find a quiet place where you will be undisturbed.

- Sit in a comfortable position, or lie down, if you prefer.
- Close your eyes and allow your body to settle into the chair or floor.
- Notice how you feel as you allow your body to relax.
- And while you are relaxing your body, begin to notice your breathing.
- Breathe naturally, and focus on how your breath goes in and out. Don't try to change your breathing, just put all of your attention on your breath. Feel your lungs and abdomen expand and contract as you breathe comfortably and easily.
- After a minute or two, begin to lengthen the time it takes to breathe in and out.
- Count slowly from one to three as you breathe in more deeply, allowing your breath to move deeper into your lungs.
- Imagine the lower third of your lungs filling up even more with fresh healing air.
- Then exhale to a slow count of three, noticing your abdomen contracting as you expel all your breath.
- Repeat the slow inhaling and exhaling for another minute or two.
- Then resume breathing normally, noticing how you feel. (More relaxed? More focused?)
- Slowly stand up and briefly stretch your neck, shoulders, and arms.

This whole experience should have taken about five minutes. And you're now ready to practice reflection—or go back to your usual activities with more clarity and energy!

FINDING YOUR REFLECTION TRIGGERS

You may already know some triggers that are effective for you. If you seek out physical exercise because it makes you feel good, then that activity is one you can use systematically to reduce stress and promote reflective thought. Even if you already practice some triggering activities, experiment with a number of others less familiar to you. For instance, if you're not the kind of person who goes to museums, make it a point to go to one, and spend at least 10 minutes looking closely at a sculpture or piece of art. Learn to knit or embroider. Take a slow walk in the woods, pausing often to notice the plants, listen to the birds, and breathe in the fresh air.

Liz DeMarais lives in the Minneapolis area and loves her work in hydraulics sales and marketing. It's a demanding industry, and when she lost her job a few years ago following a work-related injury, it would have been tempting for her to descend into fear and self-pity. But Liz has a secret weapon: She meditates three times a day, using devotions. Each morning she reads from an inspirational source, the *Daily Word*.[1] Every day has a theme, such as joy, happiness, or forgiveness. According to Liz, "I use the theme of each day as a spiritual guide for the day. I focus on the theme. I think a little bit about the day and how I'm going to use the theme, how I'm actually going to use my time and apply the theme of the day to what's most important to me." In the middle of the day, Liz takes another break. She often reads from another of her favorite inspirational books. And she reflects on how she has applied that day's theme from the *Daily Word*. Liz thinks the mid-day reflection break is really important, since it allows her to get on track if she has had any difficulty staying aligned with what she wants to accomplish spiritually. Then, at the end of the day, Liz takes a third time-out for reflection. She may read from yet another inspirational work. And she also thinks about how she is "applying my time to my values."

Liz's daily devotions have kept her focused and productive through good times and bad, through the chronic pain and stress of injury, and through a long job search. Liz is very talented, so she doesn't have trouble getting work as a contractor sales consultant. But she doesn't want just any job, no matter how lucrative. Liz cares deeply about working for a company that is aligned with her deepest values. That may take some time. Meanwhile, Liz uses her devotional practice to avoid the temptation of accepting the wrong job offer, and to make each day meaningful regardless of her external circumstances. She says: "What keeps me going is that I have these meditation points in my day. I am reflecting on when life was at its best and my life was aligned with my values. I stop and say to myself that I've always been taken care of in the past. It's all going to be fine. I know if you speak to your heart, life will be good."

MAKING REFLECTION A HABIT

When you're in the grip of a challenging financial decision, it's vital to be able to reflect on your values, your big picture, and the economic realities of whatever situation you face. Developing the habit of reflection makes it much easier to be reflective when you need it most. When those exciting financial opportunities or scary financial crises do come along, we'll be programmed to use our values to make the best possible decisions.

Cultivating a habit of reflection has an additional benefit. Most of us don't need to make financial decisions every day. However, we do need to make lots of other decisions every day. Cultivating the habit of reflection helps us align all our varied daily actions with our values and the realities of our lives and the world in which we live.

CULTIVATING THE VALUES REFLECTION HABIT

At the beginning of the chapter, I described how I reflect on my values each morning. What's important, in cultivating reflection, is to choose a regular time each day to reflect on your values and your life context. Experiment with what works best for you:

- In the shower
- While making morning coffee
- On the drive to work
- On a lunch time walk
- On the drive home from work

- During a daily walk
- In bed before going to sleep

When you choose to practice reflection is up to you. The important thing is to build a daily habit of reflecting. The more you practice reflection, the more easily you will be able to call on it when you're in the heat of a financial storm. In the Personal Values Reflection Time Exercise, I encourage you to make a commitment to build in a daily time to reflect on values. In the Daily Values Reflection Exercise, you'll have the opportunity to hone a technique for reflecting on your values.

REFLECTING ON THE BIG PICTURE

Understanding the big picture of your life creates a context in which you can make better financial decisions. Your big picture includes five major areas of life:

- Finances
- Family
- Goals
- Health
- Environment

EXERCISE: PERSONAL VALUES REFLECTION TIME

I will take time out to reflect on my values every day when I _____

_____

The values I will reflect on are:
1. _____
2. _____
3. _____
4. _____
5. _____

EXERCISE: DAILY VALUES REFLECTION

Use this technique daily to keep your values top of mind. For each of your top five or six values, say the following to yourself:
- Name the value, for example, *Family.*
- Use verbs in front of your values, to create an action orientation to each value. For example:
  - ▶ Love your family (directing yourself to put value into action).
  - ▶ I choose to love my family (making a choice to live out a value).
  - ▶ I love my family (reinforcing a desired state by visualizing it as already true).

Finances refers to your overall financial situation. How well have you prepared for the certainty of uncertainty? Is there a smart place where you can get money if you need it? Reminding yourself of the extent to which you are financially secure can go a long way toward reducing fear and anxiety about a current situation, such as a drop in the value of your mutual funds. On the other hand, reflecting on areas of financial instability could put the brakes on a risky financial opportunity that you may be excited about.

Family includes not just your immediate family, but friends and other meaningful relationships. How much personal support can they provide you? Do family members share financial responsibilities or are you the sole economic provider? Answers to these questions can help you interpret the potential effect of a negative financial event or influence your decision to pursue an attractive opportunity.

Goals are the things you want to accomplish in your life. Ideally, they are based on your values. Reminding yourself of your goals increases the likelihood that you'll make financial decisions in alignment with your goals. No matter how exciting an opportunity or how anxiety-provoking an event, reflecting on goals helps you put money in perspective.

Health includes not only your current state of well-being, but your age and health history. Reflecting on your physical strengths can help you maintain optimism about your ability to weather financial storms.

On the other hand, if your health is fragile or you have a family history of a health problem, that could temper your ability to make certain financial choices. Reminding yourself of where you are in time can also be useful. If, for instance, you are in your healthy early 40s, you can make long-term financial decisions, because there is a high probability that you will be around long enough for your stock investments to perform well enough over time for a comfortable retirement. If you are nearing or in retirement years, your health and age often dictate more caution in how you make financial decisions.

Environment represents all the factors outside your immediate control that can influence your decision-making. Environment includes the cyclical nature of economic markets, politics, and global events, the financial status of the company that employs you, the strength of the industry you work in. This book is being written during one of the most difficult economic environments in modern times. For example, extreme market volatility has characterized the new century. Reflecting on the cyclical nature of the economy and the markets can keep you from responding to market volatility and economic changes in damaging ways. Economies expand and contract. Markets go up and down. If you have prepared yourself for market volatility and other uncertainties, you will be in a much better position to weather economic storms. For instance, if you have practiced the Smart Money Philosophy introduced in Chapter 3, you will be able to tolerate unexpected financial challenges, because you're more likely to have smart places to access money and you'll be more likely to avoid impulse selling or buying.

UPDATING YOUR BIG PICTURE

Your life context may not change dramatically from week to week, but life is change, and you can expect that some aspects of your life will change over time. For this reason, I recommend that you spend a half hour or so every quarter reflecting on your big picture. If you receive a quarterly update on your 401(k) or investment accounts, use that as a reminder to set aside some time to reflect on your big picture. Reflecting on your big picture periodically will prepare you

EXERCISE: DRAWING A PICTURE OF YOUR BIG PICTURE

This activity will help you create a visual map of your big picture. Once you have completed your big picture, you can display it for a quick reminder of what to reflect on when you're reacting to a financial situation.

Materials: A large piece of paper (newsprint or drawing paper) and colored markers or crayons.

Lay your paper on a table or floor. Draw a large circle, and divide the circle like a pie into five sections.

Label each section with the five parts of your big picture:

- Finances
- Family
- Goals
- Health
- Environment

In each section, jot down the most important facts—positive and negative—that apply to that part of your life.

to reflect clearly on your context when you're actually in the throes of a highly charged financial situation.

REFLECTING DURING FINANCIAL CHALLENGES

Up to this point, our focus has been on cultivating the reflection skill in general. The more time we spend reflecting on values and our big pictures, the more access we will have to our values and life context when we need to make smart financial decisions. Armed with the reflection skill, we are ready to be reflective in those highly charged moments or during those challenging days when a financial situation is causing us either anxiety or excitement.

No matter how diligently we have practiced reflection and no matter how much time we have spent reminding ourselves of the big picture, when a challenging financial situation presents itself, we must be able to stop action, recognize our reactions, and activate our reflective capacities. When media executive Lynn Fantom was going through a divorce, her husband proposed that they both contribute to a college fund for their daughter using a particular financial vehicle. Lynn was skeptical because emotionally it was difficult to trust the advice of her soon-to-be ex. But Lynn was smart enough to recognize the emotions she was experiencing as part of her divorce. She then activated her reflection response: Lynn thought long and hard about her husband's suggestion. She thought about how much her husband cared about their daughter. She factored in the recognition that her husband was a knowledgeable financial professional whose ideas about college savings should be considered. She reflected on how important it was to her to provide for her daughter's education. And she reflected on her desire to avoid or minimize debt that might be incurred in the process of educating her daughter. Despite some emotional trepidation, Lynn signed on to the college fund. It turned out to be a wise choice. The investments within their daughter's college fund performed extremely well, and they were able to send their daughter to the college of her choice without incurring any debt.

Lynn could not be certain that the choice she made to cooperate with her ex-husband in a college fund would be successful. But by using the skills of recognition and reflection, she increased the odds of creating a situation that would benefit her daughter educationally while minimizing the financial burden of providing for her daughter's education.

We may not all need to figure out the best way to finance a child's education, but everyone has to deal at some point with a challenging financial situation. The following worksheet presents a list of the key questions we should reflect on when we are facing any significant financial situation.

REFLECTING DURING A FINANCIALLY CHALLENGING SITUATION

1. Take time to recognize your experiential triangle of thoughts, feelings, and physiology using these questions:
   - What is the financial situation that I am reacting to?
   - What are my thoughts, feelings, and physiological reactions to this situation?
   - What values should I keep in mind as I respond to this situation? What aspects of my big picture should I keep in mind as I respond to this situation?
   - What biases or untested assumptions might I be making that could affect the way I see this situation?
2. What do the answers to these questions suggest about my current situation?
3. What should I be thinking about as I decide what to do about this situation? For example:
   - How can I stay true to my values as I deal with this situation?
   - When I take my emotions out of the equation, what are the objective pros and cons of the decisions I am considering?

Although all four of the Rs are important, reflection is probably the most central to our ability to make sound financial decisions. Reflection forces us to evaluate the reliability of our automatic "outside in" responses to situations. Building our reflective skill is key to ensuring that the financial decisions we make are not impulsive, but are aligned with what we want to accomplish in our lives. And as you may have already noticed, once you reflect on what's most important to you and on the realities of the environment in which you live, it's almost inevitable that you will begin to think differently about the financial situation you face. Reflection will naturally lead to the third R—*reframing*—a new way of seeing yourself and interpreting your reality. Reflection done well and consistently will dramatically alter your sense of what is and can be true for you. In the next chapter, you'll learn how to *reframe* your situation in ways that prepare you to make remarkably smart financial decisions.

ENDNOTE

1. *Daily Word* magazine. Kansas City, MO: Unity Publishing, Unity Church.

7 | *Reframing*

When I try to convey the essence of reframing to keynote audiences and seminar participants, I often quote one of my favorite philosophers, Winnie the Pooh, who said, "I was going to change my shirt, but I decided to change my mind instead." Winnie's comment captures the essence of reframing. Often the most powerful way to promote positive change is to change our attitude, rather than our circumstances. Reframing is a cognitive technique in which we look at our situation in a different way, one that allows us to move forward in a more successful direction. When applied to financial decisions, reframing is a technique for describing our financial situation in a new way that will help us make an optimal decision. Reframing is about changing the conversations we are having with ourselves about whatever challenging situations face us.

Our typical way of interpreting reality is based on long-standing habit patterns that are burned into our brains. But, thanks to our brains' plasticity, we can change the way we view situations we face. And that's what reframing is all about—taking the results of our reflections about values, goals, and the big picture, and re-interpreting whatever financial situation we are in.

Every decision we face happens in the context of the attitudes and beliefs we have about our situation. That collection of attitudes constitutes our "frame" for that situation. And that frame, in turn, powerfully influences the actual decision we make. Often, our frames for financial situations consist of attitudes that get in the way of our ability to make smart, responsible, values-based decisions. Say, for example, you are in your 50s and you get laid off from your job. What you say to yourself about this challenging event affects everything you do—or don't do—about it. During a recession, many unemployed people say to themselves, "I'll never get a job in this market!" That attitude is their way of framing the situation they're in. Many of us know people who've adopted that frame and noticed the negative effect on their job-seeking behaviors. If you don't believe you can get a job, you are less likely to do the things that will help you get a job. During economic downturns, negative frames abound.

Each of these frames is unrealistically negative. And each of them is likely to lead to poor decisions. But not all dysfunctional frames are negative; some are unrealistically positive. For instance, people who buy things they can't afford may have frames that include attitudes such as, "I deserve this," "It's a really good price," or "I can always put it on a credit card." When our frames are unrealistically negative or positive, the likelihood that we will do something financially stupid is very high. And even if we usually see our world through a realistic lens, our realism can go out the window when we are faced with a highly charged financial situation. Emotionally stimulating events tend to tilt our usual rational frame of mind toward the unrealistically positive or negative. That's why

Situation	Frame
The stock market is down 3,000 points.	I'll never be able to retire.
My mortgage is upside down.	I'll never be able to sell my house.
My company isn't giving any raises this year.	I'm sick of working harder and getting paid less.
My college tuition bill has gone up 10%.	I'll have to drop out of school.

the skill of reframing is critical. When highly charged events threaten to highjack our thinking brains, we need a way to ensure that our way of looking at the whole situation is both realistic and positive.

Chuck and Lori's Colorado home sale (discussed in Chapter 4) illustrates how reframing sets the stage for a smart decision. As you will recall, the breakthrough came for Chuck when he was able to let go of his original frame: "We must make a big profit on any house we sell." Getting the house sold in a timely manner required that he reframe his attitude about the home's profitability to something like this: "We have made money from a number of houses we've sold in the past, and probably will do so in the future. On average and over time, we can grow equity through our real estate purchases." Chuck and Lori's story illustrates that we do not have to give up any important goal when we reframe. For example, they did not have to adopt a new frame, such as, "It doesn't matter to us whether we make money or lose money when we sell this house." Reframing doesn't force you to change what you want, only to change your beliefs about how to stay true to your long-term goals when dealing with a near-term challenge. Reframing helped Chuck and Lori adopt a more realistic and, at the same time, more optimistic picture of their real estate investments. Their ability to reframe their real estate expectations from "sell at a profit on every house" to "profit over time from selling houses as our needs dictate" was key to selling their house before the Vail real estate bubble burst. Of course, they couldn't know ahead of time that the housing market was about to deflate. But that's why reframing, along with the other three Rs, is such a powerful skill. You don't need to be able to predict the future to succeed financially. You simply have to use your financial intelligence skills, the 4Rs, to make smart, responsible, values-based decisions when it might be hard to do so naturally. By letting go of the need to make money from selling that particular house, Chuck and Lori broke even, and they avoided the loss that would have come had they waited. In addition, they were able to buy their new in-town home at a reduced rate. So even if they were only considering financial effects of their home sale, Chuck and Lori came out ahead. And that's without factoring in the benefits to their family life from having moved ahead quickly with the house sale.

UNDERSTANDING YOUR BASELINE FRAME

Most of us have a routine frame that we use to make sense of everyday life—our baseline frame. And many of us are able to maintain that perspective even when we're in a highly charged situation. But even if we can't always maintain our usual "realistically positive" frame, it's better for us to start out with a positive baseline frame. The attitudes that make up our normal baseline frame are encoded in our brain pathways. So, if events derail our baseline frame, we can use our reframing skill to get back more quickly to the brain pathways that contain our baseline frame. And that realistically positive frame is exactly what we need to make smart, thoughtful financial decisions.

Each aspect of our baseline frame shapes the way we evaluate any particular financial event—whether exciting or anxiety-provoking. For this reason, it's very useful to practice reframing daily—not only when we're excited or stressed. By consciously monitoring our routine framing, we can continuously fine-tune our frame to support wise decision-making.

Our baseline frame contains a host of attitudes and perceptions about ourselves, our abilities, and the way the world works. Our baseline frame includes the following elements:

- Whether we generally tend to view situations positively or negatively, that is, are we predisposed to think things will work out for the best or for the worst?
- Our sense of our overall well-being, including, but not limited to, finances. For example, do we generally see ourselves thriving or struggling?
- Our evaluation of how smart we are, including, but not limited to, financial matters. For example, when it comes to finances, do we think of ourselves as either "unable to balance a checkbook" or "smarter than the talking heads on CNBC?"

OPTIMIST OR PESSIMIST

All of us are predisposed to our own set of mental biases, which in turn affect our general world view. For instance, if you tend to be an optimist or pessimist, and you know this about yourself, you are especially susceptible to confirmation bias and overconfidence bias. Whether you are an optimist or pessimist, you tend to be excessively confident in your view of things. As a lifelong optimist, I've come to realize that my natural confident attitude can easily fall into overconfidence that whatever I do will result in good outcomes. I am fortunate to have enjoyed enough times when things did turn out very well for me, and that has tended to reinforce my belief that in general things will turn out well. It's important to recognize that optimism is part of my default frame, so that I can recognize a tendency to overconfidence and reflect more carefully on the objective realities of whatever financial situation I am facing.

Even if I were a pessimist, it would be equally important to recognize that I tend to be overconfident in my expectation that things will not work out well for me. If I recognize that pessimism is part of my default frame, I can be alert for my tendency to view a situation in a negative light, and reflect more carefully on the objective realities of the situation I face. When I reflect on the way things really are, as opposed to the way I tend to think things generally are, I am in a much better position to reframe my situation in a way that is appropriately optimistic and realistic.

Say, for instance, you are an optimist who considers himself good at financial matters. You tend to trust your instincts about the potential gains from investments, and you probably assume that things will turn out well for you—because they usually do. That could lead you to take short cuts in evaluating the potential risks and benefits of investments you are considering. For example, imagine you'd like to buy a vacation home in Florida. Prices have plummeted 50–60 percent in the last two years, and you now have the opportunity to buy a 2-year-old lakeside house with a gourmet kitchen within walking distance from the beach for $120,000. The price is so low, you can pay cash. It's the most beautiful place you've seen in all your house hunting.

But you are framing the opportunity in a way that could stop you from making an offer. You think, "If prices have dropped this much in two years, maybe they'll drop some more. If I wait until the fall, the market will probably be more sluggish, and we can get something even cheaper. I can't be sure I'm getting the best deal possible, until I know that we've hit the bottom of the market." So despite how much your wife loves the house, you decide not to buy it.

Six months later, the Florida market is beginning to recover. Prices are edging up. The house you were interested in earlier is in the happy hands of its new owners. You haven't found anything in your price range with the amenities you want, and you realize you'll have to spend quite a bit more to acquire your vacation dream house. Of course, there was no way to prove that the Florida real estate market was at its bottom when you were first in the market. But by uncritically holding on to your frame, "I can only buy property if I am certain it won't drop in value any further," you have lost an opportunity that could make you and your family very happy for many years to come. What if you had adopted this more optimistic, yet still realistic, frame instead? "It may not be the bottom of the market, but it has to be close. The general economy is improving, and housing will start to recover before too long. Maybe I could get something like this for a few thousand less if I wait. But this is an excellent price. And we want to own this for many years."

Of course there is simply no way to predict the future. As Ted Truscott, chief investment officer of Ameriprise Financial put it, "When you have the price, you don't have the proof. When you have the proof, you don't have the price." This applies to housing markets as well. When there are great prices on houses, there is no way to tell for certain that that is the best price, and that prices won't go down any further. But by the time you have proof that the price of a property was as low as it could get, prices have already bounced back up. That is the proof. Since you must make a decision without proof, the way you frame your situation is critical. To return to the example of buying a vacation home in Florida, the frame you adopt helps you make a decision (that is, respond) in the absence of objective proof that the timing of your purchase is ideal. If you hold on to your original frame, "I should wait until I'm sure the price wouldn't go lower," you'll be financially safe, but you and your family may miss out on a wonderful experience with the home of your dreams. But if your reflection leads you to understand that (a) you can afford this property, (b) you can afford a temporary drop in equity, and (c) your family would enjoy this unique property, then reframing can help you move forward to a decision that better suits your values. So you reframe: "Desirable island properties will not lose 100 percent of their value. People still want to vacation in beautiful warm places. The owners who bought at the height of the boom in 2006 were the ones who took the big financial hit. We could lose a little equity on paper, but it's likely that values will recover and continue to climb." If those thoughts were part of your reframing, what decision do you think you would make about that vacation home purchase?

As you can see, the way we frame a situation virtually dictates the way we respond to that situation. Framing is the cognitive activity that happens just before we launch the fourth skill, *responding*. Reframing sets the stage for making a better decision than we would have made had we responded reflexively to our emotions.

THRIVING OR STRUGGLING?

A second aspect of our baseline frame has to do with whether we think we are doing well or poorly in our financial life. Do we see ourselves as thriving or struggling? The last few years have been financially stressful for millions of Americans. Job losses, stock market volatility, and housing market declines have affected people's sense of how they are doing. But as we saw in Chapter 2, there is no direct relationship between an individual's net worth and his or her sense of financial and personal well-being. Do you think you need a lot of money to feel happy? According to a 2005 report published in the *British Medical Journal*, research conducted in Mexico, Ghana, Sweden, the U.S., and the U.K. shows similar average life satisfaction ratings despite a 10-fold difference in per-capita income across those countries. If more money doesn't bring happiness, what does?

According to research, relationships with family, friends, and the broader community are key to a satisfying life.

Several years ago, there was an article in the *New York Times* reporting on a survey conducted in the United States, which showed that to feel comfortable, people on average believed they needed twice as much as they had. "I'm in an okay spot, but I'm not comfortable." That is the type of frame that can lead to poor financial decisions. If, on the other hand, I feel like I'm thriving, I feel like I've won the game, independent of how much money I have. Whether you live in a castle or a tent, if you feel like you are thriving, you have won the game. And that is the type of frame that can protect you from making financial decisions out of discontent or feelings of desperation.

When you reflect on your values, you are likely to discover that, though your objective financial situation may be volatile, your life in the big picture is quite good. When I lost nearly 40 percent of my net worth in the recent Great Recession, I was like a lot of people who felt angry. I felt like a fool. How could I have made the investment choices I made? But reframing, along with the other Rs, saved me. I reflected on what I really cared about. Then, I reframed my situation to remind myself that the fact that I lost a lot of money didn't have to prevent me from being happy. When my grandson comes to see me, he thinks I'm the greatest thing. He doesn't quiz me about my net worth before deciding whether to love me. I've reframed my situation to remind myself that money doesn't matter beyond covering basic needs and funding what really does matter.

SHARP OR DULL

A third element of our baseline frame has to do with how smart we think we are. Most of us evaluate ourselves in terms of our general intelligence, as well as our aptitude in a host of specific life areas. Some of us are proud of our abilities in our chosen career, as parents, or in sports. We may think of ourselves as handy around the house (or not), creative (or not), and financially smart (or not). Our beliefs about our capabilities deeply affect the quality of our problem-solving and decision-making. As Henry Ford famously said, "Whether you believe you can do a thing or not, you are right." And the frame we create about our abilities often functions as a self-fulfilling prophecy about what we can accomplish, financially and personally. When we frame our situations in a positive light, we act in different ways than if we interpret them in a negative light.

We've developed an exercise on the next page for determining your baseline frame. With a good understanding of how you typically see situations, you'll be best able to reframe appropriately.

WHEN ONE DOOR CLOSES: A CASE EXAMPLE OF REFRAMING

There may be rare occasions when reframing isn't necessary, but it's always important to at least ask the question: "Is my habitual way of looking at things serving me right now?" Take for example my friend and writing partner, Kathy Jordan, who recently lost what she used to call her "security blanket client." For six years, Kathy was the free-lance editor for a monthly publication produced by a well-known business publishing company. Her fees paid the mortgage and basic bills each month. It gave her a sense of stability and the freedom to pursue other freelance work that did not pay so steadily, without worrying about the lights being turned off. Then the publisher ran into economic trouble and cancelled all of their freelance work.

Kathy was in shock. When she was able to think about her situation at all, she thought, "I don't know if I can survive!" "How could they do this to me?" and "This is terrible." Kathy then had 15 to 20 hours a week freed up, and for the first few weeks, she didn't use her time very well. Then she decided to use the 4Rs. When she did, she recognized that her attitude about her situation was making it worse. She reflected on her values, and was reminded that one of her most important ones was to help others. As she reflected, she realized that she wanted to reconnect with her earlier work helping others through coaching and consulting. Once she began to see a new direction, she then reframed her situation like this: "I may not have the financial security I would like right now, but I can use this extra time to refocus my career on helping others." Once Kathy reframed her

EXERCISE: UNDERSTANDING YOUR BASELINE FRAME

Take a few minutes to reflect on your baseline frame in the categories below:

Optimist or Pessimist

Would you describe yourself as more of an optimist or a pessimist? What is it about the way you see the world that leads you to describe yourself this way?

How do you think others would describe you?

Thriving or Struggling

Would you describe yourself as thriving or struggling? Why?

How do you think others would describe you?

Sharp or Dull

Overall, how intelligent do you think you are?

How would others rate your intelligence?

Financial Skills

How good are you at dealing with finances and making sound financial decisions?

How would others rate your financial skills?

Realism

On a scale of 1 (completely unrealistic) to 10 (completely realistic), how realistic do you think you are about yourself, your current situation, and the way the world works in general?

situation, she felt ready to act. She's created a Web site to advertise her coaching and consulting work and she is taking steps to market her services. She feels energized and excited about what lies ahead. Here's the thing about reframing: Nothing external has changed—yet. Kathy's savings account is still dwindling. But internally, everything has changed. Stay tuned.

ON THE ROAD TO A GREAT DECISION

Reframing is the launching pad for the fourth R, *responding*, and it would be impossible to reframe without the raw materials of recognizing and reflecting. Though each of the 4Rs is discussed individually, in practice they are closely intertwined. Reframing often begins while we are still in the process of recognizing our experiences. For instance, in the recognition moment, it's hard to recognize an emotion without putting a label on it. And as soon as we explicitly name an emotion, we are in effect reframing the way we understand that emotion. The emotion was one thing when we were awash in the experience of feeling it. But when we try to explain to ourselves what we have been feeling, we stop feeling the way we were feeling only moments ago. Imagine the last time you were upset about a situation at work. Then imagine what it would be like to tell a trusted colleague about your experience. Putting it into words would probably help you feel better, allow you to gain some insight into what had happened (reflection), and give you a way of seeing the situation (reframing) that was different from how you saw it while involved in the immediate experience. Recognition helps calm your physiology so you can be reflective. Then reflection gives you the raw material for reframing. By reflecting on our emotions, our values, and our big pictures, we are able to reconsider the validity of our current frames. Reflection also gives the raw material for a stronger and more useful frame. Armed with a realistically positive frame, we now feel able to tackle our financial challenges and make smart decisions about which financial opportunities we should or should not pursue.

8 | *Responding*

The ultimate purpose of the 4Rs process is to allow us to make financially intelligent decisions—smart, responsible, values-based decisions—when we are experiencing highly charged, difficult to deal with emotions. The first three Rs—*recognize, reflect,* and *reframe*—are meant to change a highly charged emotional state to a calm and productive emotional state that supports objective, unbiased thought. That is the state of mind that allows us to respond optimally to any challenging situation, financial or otherwise.

Therefore, once we've recognized our current state; reflected on our values, capabilities, and options; and reframed our situation, the next step is the fourth R—to *respond* with the best possible financial decisions. But it's not really a "final" step. Though each of the 4Rs is discussed separately in its own chapter, it's hard to separate them from one another in practice. Each R flows into the next—almost as soon as we recognize our thoughts, feelings, and physical state, we begin reflecting on what is going on in and around us. Almost as soon as we start reflecting on our values and the big picture, we begin to reframe our situation differently. And almost as soon as we reframe, we begin to think about how we want to respond. Many of us feel a strong desire to respond, that is, to act on those choices as soon as we've thought about them.

Jan Spielman heads a financial advisory practice with over $100 million in assets under management. Jan has been an active participant in our behavioral advice workshops. Jan fell in love with the simplicity and practicality of the alignment model and the 4Rs. In reflecting on her values, she realized that she wanted the values orientation of this approach to become an explicit part of her work with clients. When it comes to putting plans in action, Jan doesn't waste any time. She quickly reframed her vision of her practice to this: "Our practice will use the alignment model and the 4Rs to help our clients have the financial means to accomplish their most important life goals." Within days, Jan was busy creating a program to introduce her firm's clients to the alignment model and the 4Rs. Not only is Jan using these powerful tools herself, but she is empowering all her clients with these tools.

Jan was able to move quickly to action because her emotional state was not too highly charged or difficult to manage. Jan's emotional state was positive, her values were clear, and there was no apparent downside to modifying her approach to clients. But in the case of highly charged situations, in which we have experienced strong emotions, responding quickly—even after having taken time to recognize, reflect, and reframe—is often not the best course. Once we've worked through the first three Rs, it's tempting to assume that we are automatically ready to make an optimal decision. However, that's not necessarily true.

A WORD OF CAUTION

When practiced regularly and thoroughly, the 4Rs greatly increase the odds that we will be in the right cognitive and emotional frame of mind for smart decision-making. But, since we are not perfect, it's possible to use the 4Rs in an imperfect way. There are two major reasons for putting on the brakes before responding.

First, the 4Rs do not always produce the optimal cognitive

state for making challenging decisions. The quality of our ultimate response depends of the quality we have brought to each of the previous three Rs: The quality of our response depends on the quality of our reframing, which depends on the quality of our reflecting, which depends on the quality of our recognizing. At each step of the way, it's possible for us to make cognitive mistakes. As you'll recall, when we stop to recognize, it's important to notice how mental biases may affect our thoughts. Unexamined biases affect the quality of our reflecting, and therefore the value of the reframing we make in response to our reflecting. And if our reframing is not ideal, then the options we act on when we respond might not be in our best interest. From years of practicing recognition, I know that I have a tendency toward excessive optimism, confirmation bias, and overconfidence. Therefore, I know that I have to spend extra time when reflecting to seek out information that conflicts with data supportive of my views of the situation or initial ideas about how to respond. Unless I do that, I'm likely to create an unrealistically positive frame that leads me to pursue financial opportunities that I should reject.

Second, the 4Rs do not always produce the optimal emotional state for making challenging decisions. The 4Rs are meant to defuse emotions stimulated by outside events. However, each of the Rs can itself stimulate other emotions which occasionally get in the way of thinking at our best. As discussed in Chapter 7, my colleague Kathy Jordan experienced a big drop in freelance work in the early part of 2009. Initially she felt panicky about the drop in income, but she reframed her situation as an opportunity to shift her career direction. She felt elated about this new opportunity, and in high spirits, responded by trying to market her new services, but without a lot of success. It took Kathy a few rounds of 4Rs to recognize that she had become caught up in highly charged emotions that had been stimulated not by outside events but as a result of her own reframing. She had unknowingly flipped her frame from excessive pessimism to excessive optimism. In effect, Kathy had replaced one set of highly charged emotions with another, interfering with the quality of her response. Had Kathy taken more time to reflect and spent more time analyzing the realities of the downturn, she would have recognized that it would be as difficult to find clients for her new services as it was to find clients for her original services. Economic conditions were a big picture reality that Kathy had to deal with, no matter what kind of services she hoped to provide.

RECYCLING BEFORE RESPONDING

As tempting as it is to *respond*, once you've recognized, reflected, and reframed, there are times when it makes the most sense to postpone a response—in fact, postponing a response is frequently the best response. It's fine to consider how we want to respond, but before carrying out a decision, it's wise to repeat the first three Rs at least one more time. Responding naturally flows out of these other things, but the key is to keep cycling back among the other three Rs. As you are preparing to respond, you have to continually keep recognizing what's going on in your mind. Before you act on your choices, it's essential to make sure you have done enough problem-solving while reflecting. Look for aspects of your situation that you may have missed in your first go-around. For instance, ask yourself: "What haven't I noticed about my situation that I should consider?" or "What might be some unintended consequences of the response I am considering?"

As you're reflecting, it's also important to go back to recognition to confirm that reflecting really has put you in a calm and productive state for decision-making. For instance, how energized and how emotional are you as you reflect on your values? If you are excessively energized, you should recognize that you are still in a difficult situation to access your full faculties. As you think about your possible responses, use recognition once again to spot any mental biases. Are you looking for something to confirm your judgment? Are you choosing a course of action just because it's easy or familiar to you?

Finally, before responding, it's important to re-check your framing. Are you being realistically positive or unrealistically optimistic in your view of your situation? The value of reframing is in being able to see things clearly, with a slant toward optimism about your ability to deal with your situation. Looking at the situation through rose-colored glasses could lead you to consider responses that would be harmful to your financial or personal well-being.

Lynn Fantom, whom we met in Chapter 6, has seen the value of going full circle through the 4Rs, including the final step of acting on the basis of the three previous Rs. Lynn did a great job of using the 4Rs to set up the educational fund for her daughter. She also used the 4Rs to lower her housing costs. During her divorce, Lynn realized that the mortgage payments on her home would eat up an excessive amount of her monthly income. Though she loved the house, she reflected on her values and decided that she would sell her dream house. She's now living in a less expensive but gorgeous apartment overlooking the Hudson River. The move left her debt-free. This decision helped her feel renewed hope and optimism about the future, and also allowed her to contribute financially to some environmental nonprofits that were aligned with her commitment to the environment.

But there was one instance in which she did not adhere to the 4Rs. Lynn was wise to have worked with a financial adviser to develop a financial plan. Her adviser pointed out that her investments were over-weighted in equities. He encouraged her to make changes to her portfolio that would protect her in the event of a market downturn. But Lynn was busy. She was growing her company. She was starting a new life as a single mother. She was comfortable with the investment approach she had taken all along. She didn't take time to recognize all of what she was experiencing. She didn't reflect enough on the advice her financial adviser had offered. Her view of her finances was stuck in the past. When the stock market took a dive in the early 2000s, her net worth got hammered. Lynn learned an expensive lesson about financial decision-making. But it's a lesson that helped her make smart decisions going forward.

Each time you are considering a response to a challenging financial situation, use the worksheet on page 119 to make sure you have fully optimized the power of the 4Rs. Making time to review each of the 4Rs will enhance your financial intelligence and build confidence in your financial decision-making skills. By "recycling" through each of the 4Rs before acting on a decision, you will increase the probability of making the smartest, most responsible, most values-based decision possible.

Congratulations! You've just made a great financial decision with the help of the 4Rs. You've brought the four essential skills of recognizing, reflecting, reframing, and responding together to dramatically increase the odds that you have made a smart, responsible, values-based decision. You are steadily increasing your financial intelligence. But even the most financially intelligent people are human. We don't know everything we need to know about a financial situation. Despite our best efforts, we can at times fall prey to emotional decisions that are not in our best interest. That's why the most financially intelligent people I know tend not to go it alone. When it comes to important financial decisions, they take advantage of the expertise of financial professionals. In the next chapter, you'll discover when and how to use a financial expert to enhance your financial and personal well-being.

EXERCISE: RECYCLING THROUGH THE 4RS BEFORE RESPONDING

Before carrying through on a potential decision, use your skills of recognizing, reflecting, and reframing to validate your choice. Ask yourself these questions:

- **Recognizing**
  - ▸ What am I now thinking?
  - ▸ What am I now feeling emotionally? Am I feeling highly stimulated by my reframing or decision?
  - ▸ What is my physiological state as I consider carrying out this decision?

- **Reflecting**
  - ▸ What mental biases might be affecting my decision?
  - ▸ What information about the situation have I not considered?
  - ▸ Who might be affected by this decision—and how?
  - ▸ What possible consequences of this decision have I not considered?

- **Reframing**
  - ▸ Based on my reflecting, how realistic is my new frame?
  - ▸ Is my reframing excessively optimistic or pessimistic? (The ideal reframing is realistically optimistic.)

- **Responding**
  - ▸ Is my plan for responding based on careful reflection?
  - ▸ Is my plan for responding based on a realistically positive reframing?
  - ▸ Am I willing to defer a response until I am satisfied that my choice is smart, responsible, and aligned with my values?

Do the answers to any of these questions lead you to reconsider or modify your decision in some way? Take all the time you need to fully explore your reactions to this potential course of action.

9 | *Calling in the Experts*

When it comes to financial intelligence, Stephen Japuntich is far wiser than his years. Steve is a pre-sales engineer in the telecommunications industry in his mid-20s. He and his wife Angela are recently married and live in the Washington, D.C., area. Steve has been interested in money since he was in middle school. When Steve was in sixth grade, he was placed in an advanced mathematics class where students invested play money using a computer simulation. He loved the thrill of being able to trade and share ownership in companies. So at the ripe old age of 12, Steve talked his parents into setting up a custodial account that he would manage. His parents gave him money to get started and from that point on, he's had a great track record as a stock investor. As a young professional, he has continued to save and invest, and has taken advantage of his company's 401(k) matching program to accelerate his retirement savings.

Despite his obvious talent for managing money, Steve decided that a financial professional could help him do even better with his money. He had a demanding day job, and liked the idea of having a financial expert keep him in the loop on opportunities and trends he might otherwise miss. So Steve signed on with a broker in one of the largest investment companies in the United States. Everything seemed to be going along well, until September 2008. Steve remembers the day he realized he was not in good hands with his money manager: "My guy called up the moment the Dow tanked. He said, 'We have to sell.' I said 'Why? I am not retiring for another 40 years.' He was upset with me for not reacting. I knew right then that I couldn't trust this guy's advice. I needed an adviser who would stay calm and keep my best interests in mind." Fortunately, Steve has found such an adviser. He's got a good financial plan in place, one designed to provide financial security and growth as he and his wife begin an exciting new life together.

Steve's story illustrates the two major points of this chapter. First, it's a really good idea to have a financial adviser, even when you know a lot about the technical aspects of money and investing. Second, not all advisers are created equal. You need a certain type of adviser, one with the skills to act in your best interest at all times.

Like Steve, everyone who has money (or at least has a good income) faces a basic choice: Get some help in figuring out where to put your money or go it alone. If you practice the 4Rs, it's unlikely that you'll make disastrous financial mistakes. You'll have done your best to prepare for the certainty of uncertainty. You'll have avoided the allure of get-rich-quick schemes, and resisted the urge to buy stuff you don't need. But the 4Rs can't guarantee that you will make optimal investment decisions. The 4Rs are an essential foundation for decision-making, but they won't ensure that you get the best possible financial return on your investments or that you are prepared for the certainty of uncertainty. For that, you need the support of a comprehensive financial adviser, preferably supported by a team of content experts. And not just any financial adviser—the right financial adviser for you.

This chapter will demonstrate why it's a good idea to use the services of a financial professional. It will outline groundbreaking research on the specific characteristics of financial advisers who deliver superior financial returns on the money they manage for their clients. And it will tell you how to find the best financial adviser for your needs.

WHY DO I NEED AN ADVISER?

Most of us simply don't have the technical knowledge about investments and markets to get the best possible return on our investments. That's actually an understatement. In fact, most of us are
pretty inadequate money managers. The average investor earns far
less than the average performance of standard market indices such as
the S&P 500. Take this study, conducted annually by the financial
industry watchdog organization DALBAR: In the 20 years ending in
December 2008, the S&P 500 had a compounded return of 8.35 percent. The average equity mutual fund investor (someone like you or
me) earned an average of 1.87 percent. Clearly, the average investor
couldn't hold a candle to the S&P's performance. What's worse, the
average investor effectively lost money, since during that 20-year
period, average annual inflation was 2.89 percent.

Now why does the average investor perform so badly compared
to the average investment? A lot has to do with investor behavior,
including the kind of emotionally based decisions that the 4Rs are
intended to help prevent. But other factors come into play as well:
We may not have the technical knowledge to choose particular
investments or the investment mix that is likely to maximize our
gains. A financial adviser brings expertise in financial intelligence,
which in turn helps us avoid timing mistakes. By timing, I don't
mean that we need to find someone who is trying to time the market
(predict the highs and lows of the stock market and invest to take
greatest advantage) daily or weekly. That would be dangerous specu-
lation, and no adviser, no matter how smart, can predict the future.
But an adviser can help you consider timing decisions such as this:
Let's say you've made a 30 percent gain on a certain company stock
that is continuing to rise. Your adviser might suggest you sell that
stock and rebalance your portfolio. That way you take advantage of
your gain. Since the adviser can't predict the future, that stock may
very well continue to increase in value after you've sold it. So if you
had kept it longer, you might have made more money. But that stock
could also have gone down, in which case you would have lost
money had you not sold. The point is that you had a healthy return

you could protect by selling. Now let's put that adviser's recommendation in a broader context. Suppose the reason he was suggesting you sell that appreciated stock was because he knew you had a son who would be starting college next year, and that your stock investments were intended, among other things, to help fund your son's education. So the adviser was making a recommendation that was not only fiscally wise in general, but aligned with your unique values and goals. Left to your own devices, it might not have occurred to you to sell a stock that seemed still headed on an upward track.

Knowledge of Companies and Industry Trends. That's only one example of the many ways that a financial adviser can enhance the effectiveness of the financial decisions you make. A financial adviser also brings knowledge of companies and industry trends. She or he can provide performance data on companies in which you may be interested, as well as provide research on the factors affecting various industries that would enter into a decision to invest in a particular company or industry sector. An adviser can help you balance and rebalance your portfolio so that you minimize risk by diversifying your investments and maximize your preparation for uncertainty. Many people without advisers think their investments are more diversified than they really are. That's because the typical amateur investor has money in several mutual funds, which seem to have different investment objectives. But an expert look below the surface of those mutual funds often shows that their holdings may overlap, or that the same external risks affect these supposedly different funds.

Product Knowledge. A financial adviser can enhance your financial decision-making by using his or her product knowledge. In the financial industry as a whole, there is a lot of competition for your investment dollars. That competition has increased dramatically in the last few years, as the total market value of investments has dropped during the recent downturn and aging baby boomers start to spend their retirement funds. Banks, brokerages, and insurance companies are constantly coming up with new products to entice you to place your assets with their firms. New product features could offer significant advantages over your current vehicles, especially if your life needs are changing. But moving your money into a new product, say into a variable annuity from a mutual fund, is a very complicated decision. The annuity could give you guaranteed income later in your retirement years, while with a mutual fund, there are no guarantees about how much will be there at a given time. But the annuity may charge penalties if you need the money sooner than you originally anticipated, and the annuity will likely have higher costs than a mutual fund. A financial adviser can help you fully evaluate a financial product in terms of its ability to support your values and big-picture financial plan.

Structure and Focus on Achieving Financial Goals. Finally, a financial adviser provides structure and focus on achieving your financial goals. A financial plan is not a static document. It is a living plan that must be fine-tuned as your life circumstances evolve and as external factors such as market changes affect the value of your investments. A competent financial adviser routinely reviews your plan and investments, and may recommend changes that keep you on track to achieving your goals. For instance, my adviser Pete Silbaugh recently suggested that I increase the face value of my life insurance, since my stock investments were down. That would ensure my family would have adequate funds in the event of my death, even if less money was available to them from the proceeds of my equity investments.

THE TRUTH ABOUT ADVISER HORROR STORIES

There are bad financial advisers. The financial industry is plagued with a breed of advisers who care more about lining their pockets than helping their clients. Notorious cases such as the Bernie Madoff Ponzi scheme can make people understandably gun shy about letting anyone else have control of their money. As with any profession, there are some incompetent and/or unethical practitioners. The medical profession, for instance, includes some awful doctors. Almost everyone has run into a physician who didn't treat them well. But there's a difference in our attitude about the two professions. If we have a bad experience with a doctor, we don't give up on the profession as a whole. We don't say to ourselves, "Okay, I'll just do this surgery on myself." We look for a better surgeon. But unfortunately, many people who have a negative experience with a financial adviser do give up on the profession. They decide to manage their money themselves. That decision is another emotional one that can hurt them in the long term. The solution is not to go it alone financially, but to get an adviser who will act in your best interests. So the first step in identifying the best financial adviser for you is to recognize what makes a great financial adviser.

WHAT MAKES A GREAT ADVISER?

Jeff Haldi, a financial adviser based in Ponte Vedra, Florida, has had a rough morning. He's just dropped one of his favorite clients (and golfing buddy) Tom DeSmet. Tom and his wife Nancy have been married for 20 years and have two teenage sons. Five years ago, Tom and Nancy sat down with Jeff to develop a comprehensive financial plan. They've got the insurance they need and they have been saving for retirement and their sons' education. But Tom has gotten involved with some commercial real estate speculators. They are looking for investment partners and have convinced him that commercial property is poised for a big comeback in the near future. Tom has decided to divert a large chunk of their savings, including some earmarked for college funds, into this new investment partnership, and he wanted Jeff's help to do that. Jeff sees a disaster waiting to happen for Tom and Nancy. He's reminded Tom of his values, asked him to consider the effect on the children's education if this new investment doesn't pan out. Nothing he said to Tom would change his mind. So Jeff told Tom that he couldn't work with him anymore. He couldn't be a party to such a reckless financial decision. Tom would need to find another financial adviser to help him.

Jeff was willing to give up a lucrative and valued client because he could not in good conscience help Tom implement a plan he believed would put Tom and his family at significant financial risk. That's the kind of adviser you want, one who sticks to his or her principles and does everything possible to support your values and goals. In short, more than anything else, you want an adviser with integrity.

A recent research study conducted under the auspices of the Consortium for Research on Emotional Intelligence in Organizations confirms the importance of integrity—and a small number of other moral and emotional competencies—to your choice of a financial adviser. The study was conducted by behavioral competency experts Lyle Spencer, Ph.D., and Robert J. Emmerling, Psy.D., to measure the effect of advisers' moral and emotional competencies on their clients' portfolio performances. Researchers studied financial advisers at Ameriprise Financial who provided investment advice on baby-boomer portfolios worth between $100,000 and $500,000. Adviser moral and emotional competencies were measured through structured interviews using a behavioral event interview protocol. Client portfolio performance was measured based on the amount of assets invested continuously for a four-year period through 2004. The study found that there was a highly statistically significant correlation[1] between the prevalence of moral and emotional competencies in the advisers studied and their clients' portfolio performance. The more prevalent the presence of moral and emotional competencies in advisers, the better their clients' portfolios performed.

The study revealed that the top two competencies affecting client portfolio performance were integrity and client service orientation, followed by concern for quality and order, teamwork, and self-confidence. The advisers who demonstrated the highest scores in these competencies delivered a mean return of 24.7 percent over a four-year period (2001–2004) for their clients' portfolios, compared to a mean return of 14.3 percent by the S&P during the same period. Surprisingly, four out of the top five competencies affecting client performance were unrelated to the technical competence of the adviser. Technical competence is clearly a baseline requirement for an adviser, but the competencies that turn an average adviser into a superior one are morally and emotionally based. The first two competencies, that is, the two competencies that have the greatest effect on adviser performance, are clusters of moral competencies. The fourth and fifth most important competencies are emotional competencies. What's more, the study found that the importance of integrity is so paramount, it accounted for almost 50 percent of the difference between superior financial advisers and others. As Spencer and Emmerling concluded in the study report:

> The evidence suggests several breakthrough findings for the financial services industry. There is now statistical data to support the theory that strong moral and emotional competencies lead to helping clients make decisions to increase their investment return ... A key differentiator between financial advisers who help their clients achieve positive returns and those who help their clients achieve superior returns is moral and emotional competency.[2]

ESSENTIAL ADVISER COMPETENCIES

Let's look at each of the behavioral competencies that are strongly related to client financial results. It's important to understand what each means in practice, because these are the characteristics you should be looking for in your search for the financial adviser who is best for you.

Integrity. Integrity means a lot more than simply not lying. It means behavioral integrity such that the adviser's actions are consistent with what he or she says. Advisers with integrity "walk the talk." They communicate ideas, feelings, and intentions openly and directly, and they welcome openness and honesty from you, even when the conversation is about a difficult topic.

Client Service Orientation. Client service orientation includes a set of moral competencies related to the moral principles of responsibility and compassion. Client service orientation means that the adviser is focused on discovering and meeting your needs as a client. An adviser with high client service orientation will spend time helping you clarify your most important personal values and goals. He or she will then help you design a financial plan aligned with your values and goals.

Concern for Quality and Order. Concern for quality and order is an essential competence for high-performing financial advisers, and it is the only "hard skill" that differentiates the best advisers from the rest of the pack. Advisers who care about quality and order typically have an underlying drive to reduce uncertainty in the environment in which they operate. Advisers with this competency spend time monitoring and checking work or information. They also insist that rules and procedures that affect them and their work colleagues are clear. Clients of such advisers will notice that they are organized in their approach to scheduling and conducting transactions with them, and are diligent in completing agreed-upon work and following up with them.

Teamwork. High-performing advisers are team-oriented. They recognize the value of working cooperatively with others. They appreciate being part of a team and work well with others. In contrast, an average-performing adviser may prefer to be in charge of a group or work alone. Some aspects of an adviser's teamwork skills may not be visible to the client. Others can be clearly seen. For instance, a superior adviser will be more likely to put a client in touch with qualified professionals in other fields who can help with other needs, such as estate planning or tax accounting, and will collaborate with other professionals to serve client needs in an effective manner.

Self-Confidence. High-performing advisers are self-confident. They believe in their ability to select an effective approach to a task or problem and then effectively implement it. They are excited by challenging circumstances, and as their ability to respond quickly and effectively grows, their confidence in their opinions and decisions grows. Although they feel secure about their abilities, they do not allow their positive view of themselves to turn into arrogance.

The kind of adviser you want embodies all of these competencies. These advisers stick to their principles and do everything in their power to support your values and goals. But how do you find a really great adviser? And if you already have an adviser, how can you tell if he or she is really the best adviser for you?

FINDING A GREAT ADVISER

The first step in finding a great adviser is to recognize that no matter what, you are ultimately responsible for your financial affairs. Think of your finances as a business enterprise. Recognize that you are the CEO of your financial business. You aren't looking for someone to take charge of your finances—you are in charge. When you look for a financial adviser, you are "hiring" a chief financial officer (CFO), that is, a talented expert who will advise you and help you accomplish your financial goals. You'll want to check out their credentials, get referrals from trusted sources, and most important, ensure that he or she has the behavioral competencies (integrity, client service orientation, concern for quality and order, teamwork, and self-confidence) needed to help you.

BE CAUTIOUS ABOUT REFERRALS

When looking for an adviser, friends can be a good source of potential advisers for you to consider. But friends are probably more reliable sources of information about which advisers not to use than which advisers you can safely trust. Just because your friend is happy with his or her adviser does not necessarily mean that adviser will meet your requirements. Your friend may have different goals and requirements than you do. Your friend also might be suffering from availability and familiarity biases that keep her tied to a less-than-optimal adviser. (How many people do you think recommended Bernie Madoff to their friends?) So ask your friends a few pointed questions about their experiences with their advisers, including:

- What do you know about your adviser's credentials or certifications?
- How well do you think your adviser understands your personal values and goals?
- How has your adviser helped you prepare for possible emergencies or crises?
- What are the personal qualities you most value in your adviser?
- How satisfied are you with your adviser's help with your overall financial planning and goal achievement?
- How often do you meet with your adviser?

Thinking about your friends' answers to questions like these will often provide clues about a prospective adviser's behavioral competencies, and may prevent you from falling prey to availability bias in your ultimate selection.

CREDENTIALS

The financial services profession is quite young when compared with, say, medicine or law. Practitioners are not legally required to be certified to give financial advice. Anyone can put up a shingle as a financial adviser or financial planner. They might be competent by virtue of experience and self-study. But since there are no required standards associated with their claim to be a financial adviser, you are taking a risk that the uncertified adviser may not have adequate skills to act in your best interest. Every profession evolves over time toward standardization of credentials, and the financial advisory profession is no exception. Such standardization typically benefits both the profession and the consumer. Imagine going to a doctor who did not have his M.D. degree from an accredited medical school. Most of us wouldn't think of it. But that was exactly the case hundreds of years ago, when, if you had some ailment you went to see the corner barber. If you needed legal help prior to the 20th century, it's likely you went to a self-taught lawyer, since there were very few law schools in existence then. Even Abraham Lincoln, perhaps the most famous American lawyer of all time, honed his legal skills mostly through on-the-job training. His first law partner, William Herndon, noted:

> I easily realized that Lincoln was strikingly deficient in the technical rules of the law. Although he was constantly reminding young legal aspirants to study and "work, work," I doubt if he ever read a single elementary law book through in his life. In fact, I may truthfully say, I never knew him to read through a law book of any kind. Practically, he knew nothing of the rules of evidence, of pleading, or practice, as laid down in the text-books, and seemed to care nothing about them. He had a keen sense of justice and struggled for it, throwing aside forms,

methods, and rules, until it appeared pure as a ray of light flashing through a fog-bank.[3]

Like Lincoln, there are probably many non-credentialed financial advisers who are competent and might do a good job for you. But without a baseline credential, it's hard to evaluate their skills. Even if an adviser has a certification in the financial planning field, there's no guarantee he'll be the adviser for you. As we've seen, there are a number of critical behavioral competencies that really make for a great financial adviser. But at a minimum, certification increases the likelihood that your adviser has the comprehensive financial knowledge, technical planning skills, and sufficient experience to produce positive outcomes for you.

Types of Certifications. To increase the odds of getting sound financial help, look for an adviser with an industry certification such as Certified Financial Planner (CFP), Chartered Financial Analyst (CFA), Chartered Financial Consultant (ChFC), or Chartered Investment Counselor (CIC). To gain any of these certifications, an adviser must spend a substantial period of study and pass several grueling exams. For example, only 55–62 percent of people who take the CFP® Certification Examination pass it on their first attempt. To become certified, financial professionals also are required to have completed a number of years of qualified work in the field prior to being eligible for certification. Because of these stringent requirements, any financial adviser who has passed certification requirements has demonstrated a high level of industry knowledge, discipline, and commitment to their profession. Most CFP practitioners, ChFCs, CFAs, and CICs are well-qualified to help you consider not simply investments, but other financial vehicles such as insurance, that are essential to your ability to prepare for the certainty of uncertainty. For more information about the different types of credentials, accreditation requirements, and accrediting organizations, see the appendix.

Adherence to Regulatory Requirements. It is also important to check on the professional history of any prospective financial adviser. Professional titles or initials after advisers' names may provide assurance about their technical knowledge, but they tell you nothing about how advisers manage their businesses. Do they conduct business in an ethical manner? Do they maintain compliance with state and federal regulations? Financial professionals who sell securities and other forms of financial products are required to be licensed, and their actions are regulated by various state and federal agencies. Because they are regulated, there is a wealth of publicly available information about licensed financial professionals, including records of client complaints and any disciplinary actions taken by licensing or regulatory agencies. Ask advisers how they, specifically, are registered, and follow up online with the issuers of the advisers' certifications—with the SEC or FINRA, depending on how they are registered.

SHOULD YOU CARE HOW ADVISERS ARE PAID?

There are two things a financial adviser can get paid for: (1) giving you advice about what to do with your money, and (2) selling you a financial product such as an insurance policy or mutual fund. Based on these two sources of compensation, there are three ways an adviser can get paid: (1) paid fees for planning and advice only, (2) paid fees or commissions for selling products only, or (3) paid for a blend of advice and products. Based on those three ways of getting paid, three types of advisers have arisen. One type, which we'll call a "planning-only adviser," charges a fee for working with you to develop a comprehensive financial plan and provides ongoing advice. A planning-only adviser suggests general types of financial actions you should take, and may or may not recommend that you purchase financial products from any particular company. For instance, a planning-only adviser might suggest that you need more life insurance, and whether it should be permanent or term insurance, and quite probably would advise you on which providers offer the lowest premiums and highest ratings. They only make money for their planning and advice; they do not make an additional commission or product compensation when you implement their recommendations through purchase of a financial product.

A second type of adviser we'll call a "product-paid-only adviser." Such an adviser may give you advice (maybe even really good advice), but only gets paid if you decide to purchase a specific financial product or financial instrument through him or her. The product-paid-only adviser not only recommends a certain type of product, say a municipal bond fund, but suggests you purchase a particular company's fund, or even several no-load funds, from which the adviser makes a commission or an annual fee based on the value of the funds.

The third type of adviser, a "blended adviser," combines the first two types of advisers into one. A blended adviser will provide planning services for a fee, and, when appropriate, help you implement a financial plan (using selected financial instruments or products) for a fee.

There's been a raging debate for a number of years about which of these types of advisers is best for the consumer. A number of people interviewed for this book reported negative experiences with product-paid-only advisers who talked them into buying financial products with sales charges or fees that made money for the adviser and lost money for the client. Ethically challenged product-paid-only advisers may be tempted to advocate for investment moves that pose unacceptable risks for their client. This is the kind of scenario that has given the financial advisory profession and the investment industry in general a black eye.

However, the debate about the relative merits of planning-only versus product-paid-only versus blended advisers reflects a false choice. In my experience, I have found that the way an adviser gets paid has no bearing on whether or not a client will enjoy positive financial results. *What's really important about a financial adviser is not how they get paid but whether they care about and are capable of doing the right thing for their clients.* And that takes us right back to the moral/behavioral competencies of integrity and client service orientation. Without integrity or client service orientation, none of the categories of advisers can be trusted to work in your best interest as their client. Just because a planning-only adviser charges you, for example, $800 for a financial plan or $300 per hour, doesn't make that plan or relationship an optimal one for you. The planning-only adviser is not necessarily more objective or more thoughtful about your financial situation because he or she is paid only for the planning and advice. In fact, since he's only paid for planning and advice, he doesn't suffer any financial loss if your implementation of the plan doesn't work out so well. He may not even push you hard enough to implement the plan.

And just because a product-paid-only adviser recommends a particular financial product that she'll get paid for selling, doesn't mean it won't be a good investment for you. If your product-paid-only adviser has high integrity and client service orientation, she will make recommendations for particular products that are aligned with your values and optimally prepare you for the certainty of uncertainty. Similarly, the blended adviser is not necessarily more competent than the other two types. In all of the above categories of compensation, you should request information on any real or potential conflicts of interest.

In summary, the nature of the adviser's reward system is far less important than the nature of their moral and behavioral orientation. That said, I do have a bias about which adviser to choose. I recommend a blended approach because I believe it is in my best interest to pay for ongoing advice and to be able to implement that advice using the same adviser whenever possible. I believe that an adviser should be compensated for whatever services he provides, planning or products or both. That ensures that an adviser is being fairly compensated for his or her expertise, whether it's advice- or product-related. What I'm recommending is really no different from going to my primary care doctor who happens to be an internal medicine specialist. If my doctor discovers I have a problem, I'd prefer that she help me fix it. If my problem requires expertise that my doctor lacks, then I'm happy to have her refer me to a specialist and hopefully that specialist is someone on her team. But whenever possible, I like to have the people who give me advice help me implement that advice.

EVALUATING ADVISER COMPETENCIES
No matter how loudly a friend sings an adviser's praises, make a commitment to personally screen your prospective adviser or advisers.

Interviewing more than one adviser can open your eyes to their respective advantages and disadvantages, thus giving you more information on which to make your hiring decision. If you are considering more than one adviser, schedule a meeting with each of them. When you arrive, keep in mind that you are in charge of the meeting (after all, you're the CEO!). Remember that you are making a hiring decision. After introductions, let the adviser know that you have some questions you'd like to ask after he gives you a general introduction to his practice.

On the next two pages you'll find a list of 10 questions that will give you a pretty comprehensive idea of the behavioral competence of the adviser you are considering. Asking even a few of these questions will give you better information about the skills that really matter than you could ever learn during a typical introductory meeting with a prospective adviser.

When you look at these questions, you'll see that many ask the adviser to tell you about specific situations they've dealt with. This approach is meant to give you more accurate and detailed information about what an adviser *actually does*. The question format makes it harder for an adviser to tell you what he thinks you want to hear.

Choosing the right financial adviser takes time and care. It's not a simple matter to figure out in advance whether an adviser has the integrity and commitment to service that will support your goals in good times and bad. But the rewards—both financially and personally—can be enormous. Georgianne Meade knows a lot about the difference a great adviser can make. For the last 35 years, Georgianne has worked in a variety of professional positions at a San Francisco medical school. Georgianne's relationship with her adviser has evolved into a rich and rewarding one:

> My adviser is Saki Kono, and we've been with her for 11 years. I have great faith in her. But before we signed on with Saki, I did my homework. I did a lot of interviews with advisers and heard lots of stories. When my husband Paul and I first began to work with Saki, we didn't turn over the management of all of our

TEN QUESTIONS TO ASK A FINANCIAL ADVISER CANDIDATE

1. What are your most important values? *(This can provide information on an adviser's* general orientation to values. *Beware of an adviser who hems and haws when you ask this question. An adviser who is in touch with his or her own values is also more likely to act in ways that support your values.)*

2. What is the one thing your clients say most often about you? *(Best responses: "honest," "trustworthy," "keep my promises," "do what's best for them in the long term," all of which speak to* integrity.*)*

3. Can you tell me about a time when a client wanted to make a financial decision that you didn't think was in their best interest? How did you handle that? *(This can provide information on an adviser's* integrity, *that is, is he or she willing to stick up for his or her principles even if it may cause conflict or result in lost business?)*

4. Can you tell me about a situation in which you made a mistake dealing with a client? How did you handle that? *(This can provide information about an adviser's* integrity, *for example, was he or she willing to admit the mistake to the client? Also look for non-verbal behavior, such as squirming or looking away, which could indicate that you are not getting a truthful story.)*

5. Tell me about how you handle your working relationship with your most difficult client. What do you do that's different from how you act in your relationship with your favorite client? *(This can provide information on* client service orientation, *for example, the ability to provide good service even when clients are difficult; doing what's best regardless of personal feelings.)*

Continued on page 138

money. When I got some money from my father, it felt like too much of a burden to figure out what to do with it, so we asked Saki to help. We took baby steps, and over time, gave Saki more and more of our money to manage. She has done very well for us financially, and that has made me more and more confident. One

TEN QUESTIONS TO ASK A FINANCIAL ADVISER CANDIDATE *(CONTINUED)*

6. What services do you personally provide that I might not expect from another adviser? *(Can provide information on* client service orientation.)

7. How do you make sure that your clients always know where they stand relative to their financial and life goals? *(This can provide information about an adviser's* concern for quality and order, *especially if the adviser seems animated and provides examples of his or her personal involvement in providing information, rather than speaking only about what the firm does.)*

8. Can you tell me about a situation in which you worked with another professional inside or outside your firm to help meet a client's needs? Who did you work with and what was your relationship with him or her like? *(This can provide information on the adviser's* teamwork. *How easy is it for the adviser to recall such a situation, and how involved did he or she seem to be?)*

9. How have you personally responded to market volatility, and how have you communicated your thoughts and feelings about market volatility to clients? *(This can provide information on an adviser's* self-confidence. *A good adviser will have emotions like anyone else, but will express confidence in his or her ability to help you prepare for any life eventuality.)*

10. What kind of return can I expect if I asked you to manage my investments? *(This can provide information on an adviser's* integrity. *No adviser can predict the future, so beware of promises to produce a high rate of return. Also, look for responses that indicate the adviser does not think of himself or herself solely as a money manager, but also sees his or her role as helping you prepare for a variety of life events and helping you make decisions that support your values and goals.)*

thing that's really important to me is that she is very calming. My husband and I have different ways of reacting to money issues. When the stock market went down a lot last year, Saki walked us through what it really meant for us and helped my husband worry less.

Saki is more than a money manager for Georgianne and Paul, she's a trusted adviser. Recently, Georgianne learned that her work hours at the medical school were being reduced to three days a week as part of a cost-savings program. Georgianne felt extremely worried about her future:

I started picturing a homeless woman I used to see on my drive to work. She used to push her shopping cart from Sausalito to Mill Valley, a four-mile walk. It took her all day to get there, going through the trash cans to find something to eat. When my hours were cut, I thought, just for a minute, "That could be me." But instead of totally freaking out, the first thing I did was call Saki. I told her the situation. She asked us to come in and meet with her right away. Saki helped us reflect on all the implications for our lives. We started to make up a new budget and find opportunities where we could save. Thanks to Saki, we figured out that I could retire and we could still live comfortably—and that I could probably make more money consulting.

In addition to helping the Meades plan for reduced income, Saki has collaborated with the couple's attorney and accountant to make sure they are prepared for the future: They've updated their health-care directives and powers of attorney, and prepaid for their funerals. As Georgianne says, "It's quite a network." The relationship that Saki Kono has with Georgianne is a credit to both of them. Georgianne did her homework and knew what to look for—someone with high integrity and commitment to her clients. Saki is clearly an extraordinary adviser. She cares deeply about her clients' well-being in all areas of their lives. Saki may be exceptional, but fortunately there are many other financial advisers with the competencies and personal qualities that can make your life better. Now it's up to you to use the tools you've learned here to go out and find a great adviser.

ENDNOTES

1. The correlation was $p < .001$, meaning that the chance of the research not producing valid results was less than 1 in 1,000.
2. Emmerling, Robert J., Lyle Spencer, *et al.* 2007. "Morally and Emotionally Competent Financial Advisors Deliver Superior Client Service and Portfolio Performance." White Paper. Consortium for Research on Emotional Intelligence in Organizations (June 7).
3. This research was funded by Ameriprise Financial Inc. In addition to the principal investigators, three other certified behavioral event interviewers (including the author) conducted the behavioral event interviews of advisers. Interviewers, who were certified in the behavioral event interview method, had no knowledge of advisers' client portfolio performance. Lennick Aberman Group provided editorial assistance in the preparation of the white paper.
4. Herndon, William H. 2006. *Herndon's Lincoln.* University of Illinois Press. 209.

10 | *Your Money and Your Life*

Bob Shanley is undeniably affluent. He and his wife Andrea live in a lovely home in upscale Milton, Massachusetts. They've raised three wonderful children. Bob could have a lot more money and be a lot less happy than he is today. But he made some choices, with the full support of Andrea, to use their money—and his time—in some remarkable ways.

Bob was only 6 years old when his father died, leaving his mother, Laura, to care for their three sons. Laura brushed up on her bookkeeping skills and went back to work. No matter how tired Bob's mother was each night, she came home from work and made her boys a delicious meal. Money was tight, but he didn't realize that until much later. What he did know all those years was that he had a strong and loving mother who made sure her boys grew up with a good education, good values, and lots of love.

Bob made good use of his upbringing. By his early 30s, Bob was a successful investment analyst and head of research for a Boston investment management firm. When the firm was bought out by a larger company, Bob, by then an equity partner, received a three-year payout from the acquisition. Bob and Andrea used the first year's payout to pay off the mortgage on their home. When the second year rolled around, Bob and Andrea felt strongly that they should use the money to help others. Bob researched area homeless shelters and heard about Project Hope, a shelter with a strong reputation for helping homeless mothers gain job skills and start independent lives. Bob and Andrea looked up the address of the shelter and mailed them a substantial amount of appreciated stock. The shelter staff was flabbergasted to receive such a sizable contribution out of the blue. Each year since then, Bob and Andrea have continued to contribute to Project Hope. But thanks to Bob and Andrea's support, which supplements funding from government agencies, charitable foundations, and other major donors, Project Hope has morphed from a single homeless shelter to a $5 million nonprofit multiservice agency whose mission is to get people out of poverty.

When Bob retired in his mid-50s, he was determined to use his financial independence to make a positive difference in the lives of the poor. His first post-retirement job was as a driver picking up donations for a local charity "Cradles to Crayons," which provides needed supplies and clothing for underprivileged children. These days, he is their equipment specialist, cleaning and safety-checking donated baby equipment, such as strollers, car seats, and playpens so they meet current government safety standards. Bob also has become a member of the board of Project Hope and serves on its financial committee, dealing with retirement plans for the agency's employees. Bob's post-retirement career is one in which he is committed financially, intellectually, and physically to the goal of eliminating poverty in the region where he lives. Recently, Bob realized that the philanthropic work he does is a tribute to his mother. Laura Shanley's youngest son saw how hard it can be to raise children who grow up with good values, becoming self-assured and financially independent. That is what Bob wants for all children. Bob is more than willing to use his time and money to make that happen.

MAKING MONEY MATTER

So far this book has focused on helping you enhance your financial intelligence—your ability to make smart, responsible, values-based decisions in the face of competing and difficult emotions. Let's imagine that you are now following two important rules of financial intelligence: (1) prepare for the certainty of uncertainty, and (2) always make decisions based on your values. Hopefully you also are practicing the four skills of financial intelligence: Recognize, Reflect, Reframe, and Respond. If you've been doing all that, then you are probably already seeing positive results in your daily life—you are spending time and money more wisely; you feel more confident in your ability to weather economic and personal storms; and you are seeing yourself move closer to your most cherished goals. These gains are real and significant. But you now have the opportunity to reap even bigger rewards from your newfound financial intelligence. That's because developing your financial intelligence has laid the foundation for a life of deeper personal meaning. In the end, financial intelligence isn't really about finance. In the words of the book's title, it's about making values-based decisions with your money and your life. As important as money can seem, especially when you think you don't have enough, money in and of itself doesn't really matter much. As *Boston Globe* journalist Drake Bennet pointed out:

> Psychologists and economists have found that while money does matter to your sense of happiness, it doesn't matter that much. Beyond the point at which people have enough to comfortably feed, clothe, and house themselves, having more money—even a lot more more—makes them only a little bit happier. So there's quantitative proof for the preaching of St. Francis and the wisdom of the Buddha. Bad news for hard-charging bankers; good news for struggling musicians.[1]

But money *can* matter. In fact, money should matter. Money should be used to enrich our lives, not just our bank accounts. We make money matter when we use it to make our lives matter—in two important ways:
- We make money matter by the way we go about making money

- We make money matter by what we do with money after we've earned it

WHAT YOU DO TO MAKE MONEY

Most of us need to work to earn a paycheck. And it's probably no surprise that only a third of workers are really happy with their jobs, or that 20 percent of us really dislike our jobs. What may be less obvious is the kind of jobs that make us happy and fulfilled. According to the National Opinion Research Center:

> Firefighters, the clergy, and others with professional jobs that involve helping or serving people are more satisfied with their work and overall are happier than those in other professions, according to results from a national survey.
>
> "The most satisfying jobs are mostly professions, especially those involving caring for, teaching, and protecting others and creative pursuits," said Tom Smith, director of the General Social Survey (GSS) at the National Opinion Research Center at the University of Chicago.
>
> "Work occupies a large part of each worker's day, is one's main source of social standing, helps to define who a person is, and affects one's health both physically and mentally," Smith states in a published report on the study. "Because of work's central role in many people's lives, satisfaction with one's job is an important component in overall well-being."[2]

The evidence is clear. We are happiest when we make money by serving others. It's no coincidence that serving others is aligned with the moral principles of responsibility and compassion that are essential components of our value systems. When we serve others, we recognize our responsibility to help others besides ourselves; we also demonstrate our compassion for the needs of others beyond ourselves. Therefore, we make money matter when we align our career choices with our principles and values. Making money in a way that matters—through service—is not a luxury; it is a necessity. Making money in a way that matters is a win-win, since when we serve others, we make ourselves happy in the process. It's a healthy way to be selfish and selfless at the same time.

Some people might argue that they can't afford to work at a service-oriented job or that they can't find the kind of job that would allow them to serve others. That may be true in a very few cases. Most of us can work at jobs that include service, if we understand what service is really all about. There are many ways to serve others, beyond the obvious jobs in the so-called helping professions. We always have the choice to serve others, whether they are vulnerable individuals, groups with certain needs, or society in general. There is a story that has been told over the years about a visit President John F. Kennedy made to a NASA location. He happened to notice a man holding a mop. Kennedy shook the man's hand and asked him what he was doing. The man replied, "Mr. President, I'm sending a man to the moon." There are many ways to serve, and as this story illustrates, our ability to connect what we do to make money with a higher purpose helps everyone including ourselves.

Noted 18th century economist Adam Smith helped people understand that it was in their interest to serve the interests of others,[3] a concept best described as "enlightened self-interest." You can be a marketing specialist helping consumers understand how your company's product can improve their lives. You can be a landscape gardener at a hospital that saves lives. A majority of places of employment, whether profit or nonprofit enterprises, offer opportunities to serve. That said, not all businesses produce products or offer services that are worthy of your commitment and effort. For example, there are companies that make products that are demonstrably hazardous to human health. If at all possible, you should avoid working for a company that offers a questionable product or service. Such businesses don't deserve to have employees. There are a few businesses that should go out of business because of the harm they do to society. If you choose to work for a business that makes a profit despite the harm it does to society, you will discover how demoralizing it can be to earn money in a way that is out of alignment with your values.

WHAT YOU DO WITH THE MONEY YOU MAKE

If you are using your financial intelligence, the odds are good that you will be able to make more money than you must spend. That's because you've learned to save and overcome the urge to spend on items that are not aligned with your values. So once you've used money to satisfy your personal needs and meet your responsibilities, what *should* you do with your money? Research shows that the same things that make you happy on the job also make you happy outside the job—serving others. Research now shows that the way we spend our money has a profound effect on our level of happiness. Psychologists Elizabeth Dunn, Lara Akin, and Michael Norton authored a number of studies showing that people experience greater happiness when they spend money on others than on themselves. For instance, in a survey of 632 Americans, they found that the more people spend on charitable donations and gifts, the higher their levels of self-reported happiness. To ensure that these results weren't a result of charitable people being happier to begin with, the researchers conducted a follow-up study. They gave college students $20, then randomly told them either to: (1) use the money to pay a bill, an expense, or a gift for themselves, or (2) buy a gift for someone else or give it to a charity. The second group subsequently reported significantly greater levels of happiness than the group that spent the money on themselves.[4]

Though I haven't seen research to prove it, I believe that the way we contribute money to others makes a difference to our overall sense of fulfillment. When Amy and Dale Harbison decided to construct housing for struggling single mothers, they discovered how rewarding it was to see the results of their efforts in the rebuilt lives of poor families they helped. My wife Beth Ann and I have had a similar opportunity to help disadvantaged teenagers through our involvement in A Better Chance (ABC). ABC is a nonprofit organization that places gifted but underprivileged minority students in top college preparatory and high schools throughout the country. ABC students live in supervised group homes in communities that have excellent schools. Since they live far from home, they spend regular time with local host

families. In addition to serving on the board of the Minneapolis chapter, Beth Ann and I have served as "host parents," helped raise money for housing expenses, and together with Steve and Susan Kumagi of Edina, Minnesota, have funded a college scholarship for a deserving ABC student. Beth Ann and I have the luxury of contributing to this and several other worthwhile community-based programs, thanks to a lifetime practice of values-based financial decision-making.
Cultivating financial intelligence by preparing for the certainty of uncertainty and practicing the 4Rs has given me the time and financial resources to invest in nonprofit organizations that make a positive difference in the lives of young people. The satisfaction that Beth Ann and I get from our community involvements is priceless.

MONEY WELL SPENT

Using money to serve others is clearly an important part of being aligned with our principles and values. That doesn't mean that we must be so puritanical that we never spend money on ourselves. But if we want to maximize our level of happiness, we should spend our money on experiences, not material goods. Buying experiences creates long-lasting memories that increase our sense of well-being. For instance, call to mind an enjoyable event you've experienced in the last year, say dinner out with friends or a relaxing vacation. Rate your level of happiness as you recall this memory on a scale of 1 to 10, with 10 being very happy. Now think about a material object you've purchased in the last year, say a piece of jewelry or a flat-screen TV. Rate your level of happiness as you recall that purchase. If you're like most of us, you feel happier thinking about the experience than the material object. Why? When we buy "stuff," we get used to having it, and it no longer brings us the amount of pleasure that we experienced when we first bought it. Memories, on the other hand, become more pleasurable over time. We tend to remember the most positive aspects of the experience, perhaps even embellish our experience, while the negative aspects of the experience, say a gut-wrenching plane ride to a wonderful vacation destination, tend to fade in our memory over time. Behavioral economists have verified this phenomenon. Their studies demonstrate that what they call "conceptual consumption" gives people far more fulfillment than "physical consumption."[5]

So, contrary to conventional wisdom, money can buy happiness—if you use it to create positive experiences for yourself and others. That's the ultimate value of practicing financial intelligence.

HELPING OTHERS MAKE *THEIR* MONEY MATTER

Family. Many of us have learned the hard way about the hazards of emotionally based financial decisions. Without the benefit of financial intelligence, we may have made financial choices that jeopardized our most important goals, spent money we didn't have (courtesy of our credit card companies), or spent money we did have on material stuff that did nothing to serve our long-term happiness. But now we know better. Neuroscientists and behavioral economists have helped us understand why we make bad choices. This book presents a straightforward behavioral approach to overcoming our biological tendency to make poor money choices. Financial intelligence involves following two basic rules and practicing four concrete skills. There is no rocket science involved—just a willingness to do what it takes to build your financial intelligence.

Now how do you get the rest of your family on board? If you are a parent, you have modeled your way of managing finances—for good and ill. In effect, you have taught your children how to behave with and around money. You may not think they are paying attention, especially if they are teenagers, but they absorb and eventually emulate everything you do. If you bought things with plastic, you taught them that all they need is a plastic card to get something they want. If you go to the ATM without explaining how it works, you may have taught your children that there is a machine which can provide free money. If you talk a lot about "stuff" you want to have, you have trained children to value stuff. If you bought a lot of stuff, whether you could afford it or not, you taught them that getting stuff is a desirable way to spend time and money. If your children asked you for a lot of stuff and you consistently felt obligated to buy it for them, you taught them that there is an unlimited source of funds—you—for whatever stuff they happen to want. These hypothetical examples reflect how a big percentage of middle class and wealthy parents actually deal with money around their children.

Our children have learned to be generous in spirit and with money. My son Alan is a financial adviser and wants to help people with their money. Probably not surprisingly, he practices everything I preach in this book with his clients. My younger daughter Joanie is a psychology major and is interested in education. She will be graduating at the time this book is published and is likely to pursue a graduate degree in her interests. My older daughter Mary graduated with a degree in sociology and is also likely to get her master's degree and pursue becoming a counselor. All three of them are pursuing careers in which the process of making money matters. My wife Beth Ann has taken the lead in helping them establish financial discipline. When they want something, she asks, "What can you afford and what can't you afford?" From the way we have made and used money, and from the charitable work we have supported, our children have had an opportunity to see and understand the process of making money matter. Alan has also seen the process of making money matter through his mother Eme, who is director of an assisted living facility, certainly a profession in which she makes a difference. From our behavior as parents, they have seen generosity with money and time.

They have also seen consumption. As parents, we are not perfect, so they have not seen perfect financial decisions all the time. Knowing what I know now, I would have done a better job of getting them to think about saving earlier in their lives. These days I encourage my children, and my friends' children, to allocate their money in several ways—to spend, to save, and to give to others in need. When my friend Spenser Segal's son Adam had his sixth birthday, I gave him $60. I said, "Here's $20 for you to spend, $20 for you to give away, and $20 for you to save." Beth Ann and I try to teach our kids that how you make money matters, and that when you have money, you can do things with it besides treat yourself. As a result our children all have savings accounts, life insurance, and investment accounts.

A recent severe economic downturn may have inspired some parents to change the messages they are sending kids about money. But even if we are finally learning how to say "no" to ourselves and our kids, that won't be enough to help the next generation develop the financial intelligence they need to thrive in an uncertain future. *Knowing* what's best for us financially is different from *behaving* in a way that's best for us.

So how do we change our children's behavior around money? Begin at the beginning. Talk to your children about your values, and ask them about theirs. There are some wonderful tools to help kids get a handle on their values. Let them know that the purpose of money is to help us accomplish whatever is most important in our lives. Then give them some examples of how your values affect spending decisions that you make. For instance, if one of your values is making sure your children can get educated as far as they need to go, explain college savings plans and discuss what kind of spending might be reduced in order to fund their college accounts.

Next, teach your children the 4Rs. By the time Adam Segal was 9 years old, he knew the 4Rs and the alignment model. Children can practice the 4Rs, not just with their allowance money, but in many challenging areas of their lives—school relationships, how to balance study and play time, even dealing with you!

Finally, educate children about the real purpose of money—to meet our basic personal needs and provide meaningful experiences for ourselves and others. Sell them on the value of experiences over stuff by spending time with your children on activities that don't involve major money expenditures—family game night, sports, and community service projects.

CHANGING OUR MONEY CULTURE

Steve Lear is the Twin Cities-based financial adviser who has volunteered for over 40 disaster recovery operations in the United States. You would think that Steve's busy financial services practice and his disaster recovery work could keep him more than busy. But you would be underestimating Steve. In his "spare time," Steve is heavily involved in the *Financial Matters Initiative* of BestPrep, a Minnesota-based nonprofit that provides programs in business, career, and financial literacy skills to high school students. To date, they have contributed to the financial intelligence of over one million students through experiential learning and mentoring by business leaders to help prepare students for the economic realities they will face. One such program is the Stock Market Game, a classroom-based simulation that helps students learn the basics of investing. The effect of this kind of program can be seen in the last chapter's story about Stephen Japontich, whose successful financial life began with such a program when he was a young student.

Steve Lear's philanthropic commitments demonstrate how smart financial choices throughout your life can give you the time and resources to devote yourself to causes that are important to you. If you are living paycheck to paycheck, it's hard to carve out time and energy for activities that support non-financial values. Lynn Fantom is the busy media executive whom we met earlier in the chapter on reflecting. Lynn is deeply committed to nature and the environment. Her special love is Acadia National Park, which is a unique and pristine area in northeast Maine. Lynn spends as much time in Acadia as possible. She also commits her professional skills and her money to support the preservation of Acadia so that it can be enjoyed by future generations. Lynn describes her passion about Acadia in this way: "I'm promoting family vacations in places like Maine with my time and my money. It's very cool and makes me feel happy. I publish a Web site called ouracadia.com and that's where I place free ads for societal good. This is important to me and this is important to do." Lynn's wise financial choices over the years have allowed her the time and money to advance a cause that is dear to her heart.

A few years ago, my business partner Rick Aberman and I conducted a workshop at the Wharton School for international MBA students. Rick and I asked the group, "What will you do with the financial opportunities that will come to you as a result of becoming a Wharton MBA graduate?" Their first two responses especially inspired me: "We will be able to create meaningful jobs all over the world and be able to pay workers meaningful wages," and "For those who are unable to help themselves financially, we will be able to help them with our financial resources." That is the promise of financial intelligence. That is what living in alignment and on purpose is all about. That is what is possible when we come together as a global community to practice the 4Rs. That is what we can do together to make money truly matter. Whether it's helping ourselves, our families, our communities, or our world, the 4Rs—recognizing, reflecting, reframing, responding—are essential tools for living well and ensuring that everyone and everything we value has the resources needed to grow and bloom.

ENDNOTES

1. Bennet, Drake. 2009. "Happiness: A Buyer's Guide." *The Boston Globe* (August 23): www.boston.com/bostonglobe/ideas/articles/2009/08/23/happiness_a_buyers_guide.
2. Jeanna Bryner. 2007. "Survey Reveals Most Satisfying Jobs." *LiveScience* (April 17): www.livescience.com/health/070417_job_satisfaction.html.
3. Wood, John C. 2004. *Adam Smith: Critical Assessments Volume I.* Routledge Publishing. 352.
4. Dunn, Elizabeth, Lara B. Aknin, and Michael I. Norton. 2008. "Spending Money on Others Promotes Happiness." *Science* 21 (March) 319.5870: 1687–1688.
5. Ariely, Dan, and Michael I. Norton. 2009. "Conceptual Consumption." *Annual Review of Psychology* 60: 475–99. www.people.hbs.edu/mnorton/ariely%20norton%202009.pdf.
6. Van Boven, Leaf, and Thomas Gilovich. 2003. "To Do or to Have? That Is the Question." *Journal of Personality and Social Psychology* 85, 6: 1193–1202. www.psych.cornell.edu/sec/pubPeople/tdg1/VB_&_Gilo.pdf.

Appendix

FINANCIAL PLANNER DESIGNATIONS, ACCREDITING ORGANIZATIONS, AND REQUIREMENTS

Certified Financial Planner™ (CFP®)—Those with the CFP certification have demonstrated competency in all areas of finance related to financial planning. Candidates complete studies on over 100 topics, including stocks, bonds, taxes, insurance, retirement planning, and estate planning.

Accrediting Organization: The program is administered by Certified Financial Planner Board of Standards Inc.

Accreditation Requirements: CFP® certificants must pass the comprehensive CFP® Certification Examination, pass CFP Board's Candidate Fitness Standards, agree to abide by CFP Board's *Code of Ethics and Professional Responsibility,* which puts clients' interests first, and comply with the *Financial Planning Practice Standards,* which spell out what clients should be able to reasonably expect from the financial planning engagement.

Web Site: www.cfp.net

Chartered Financial Analyst (CFA®)—Those with the CFA designation have extensive knowledge in accounting, ethical and professional standards, economics, portfolio management, and security analysis. CFA charterholders tend to be analysts who work in the field of institutional money management and stock analysis, not financial planning. These professionals provide research and ratings on various forms of investments.

Accrediting Organization: CFA Institute (formerly the Association for Investment Management and Research [AIMR]).

Accreditation Requirements: To obtain the CFA charter, candidates must successfully complete three difficult exams and gain at least three years of qualifying work experience, among other requirements. In passing these exams, candidates demonstrate their competence, integrity, and extensive knowledge in accounting, ethical and professional standards, economics, portfolio management, and security analysis.

Web Site: www.cfainstitute.org

Chartered Financial Consultant (ChFC)—Individuals with the ChFC designation have demonstrated a thorough knowledge of financial planning. Like those with the CFP certification, professionals who hold the ChFC charter help individuals analyze their financial situations and goals.

Accrediting Organization: The American College

Accreditation Requirements: In addition to successful completion of an exam on areas of financial planning, including income tax, insurance, investment, and estate planning, candidates are required to have a minimum of three years of experience in a financial industry position.

Web Site: www.theamericancollege.edu/subpage.php?pageId=254

Chartered Investment Counselor (CIC)—Designation implies that adviser has significant experience with investment counseling and portfolio management, and that the adviser is held to a higher set of ethical standards.

Accrediting Organization: Investment Counsel Association of America Inc. (ICAA)

Accreditation Requirements: Must first obtain a CFA, then be employed be a member of the Investment Counsel Association of America (ICAA) and have five years of related work experience. Web Site: www.icaa.org

SOURCES

Financial Planning Association—www.FPAforfinancialplanning.org/FindaPlanner/ChoosingaPlanner/
  FinancialPlanningDesignations
Certified Financial Planner Board of Standards Inc.—www.cfp.net
CFA Institute—www.cfainstitute.org
The American College—www.theamericancollege.edu/subpage.php?pageId=
Investment Counsel Association of America, Inc. (ICAA)—www.icaa.org

Acknowledgments

This book could never have been written without the influence of a large number of people. I am indebted to my colleagues at the Lennick Aberman Group, including Rick Aberman, Ph.D.; Chuck Wachendorfer; Judy Skoglund; Kay May; Jim Choat; Jim Jensen; Ben Smith; Chris Ambrose; and Elaine Larson, each of whom has contributed to the development of LAG's Behavioral Advice Services.

I am enormously grateful to everyone who allowed us to share their stories in the book. I also appreciate those who generously shared their experiences and insights about values-based financial decision-making, but who do not appear by name in the book: Kathy Arneson, Michael and Judy Ayers, Tim Barzen, Travis Chaney, William Donovan and Marie Cosgrove, John Ekman, Richard and Ann Evers, Adina Flynn, Harry Hunt, Matt and Patty Jackel, John Karpinsky, Donna Krone, Marianna Leuschel, Kathi Long, Stewart and Vickie McLauchlan, Bill and Susan Metzger, Mike Metzger, George Papadoyannis, Cindy and Al Rosby, John Schubert, Michael Scott, Sharyn Solish, Dana Wales, Tony Whitbeck, Tom Winkels, and Greg Wright.

Special thanks go to the following individuals who have championed the behavioral advice model on which this book is based within their organizations: Roger W. Arnold, Senior VP and Chief Distribution Officer, Wealth Enhancement Group; Jeff Dekko, CEO, Wealth Enhancement Group; Bernie De La Rosa, CFP®, ChFC, CRPC, CLU, Advisor Consultant, Ameriprise Financial; Randy Ehleringer, CFP®, Franchise Consultant, Ameriprise Financial; John Greiber, Group Vice President, Ameriprise Financial Midwest; Jack Handy, CEO, FINC; Joe Hart, SVP & Director Retail Investment Sales, ING Investment Management; Bruce Helmer, President, Wealth Enhancement Group; Terry Hinnendael, CFP®, Franchise Consultant, Ameriprise Financial; Ken Krei, President, Wealth Management Group, M&I Bank; Mark Ledson, CFP®, Group Senior Partner, Thrivent Financial for Lutherans; Jeff Marshall, ChFC, Senior Franchise Consultant, Ameriprise Financial; Kim Mickelson, VP Financial Planning and Advice, Ameriprise Financial; Frank Mossett, Region Vice President, Ameriprise Financial New England; Kirk Osborne, CFP®, Franchise Consultant, Ameriprise Financial; Debra Pallazza, First American Funds; Kris Petersen, SVP & General Manager Financial Planning and Advice, Ameriprise Financial; Tony Pizzo, CFP®, Franchise Consultant, Ameriprise Financial; Tom Schinke, Financial Consultant, Thrivent Financial for Lutherans; Joe Schlidt, VP, M&I Bank; Spenser Segal, CEO, ActiFi; and Jim Thomsen, Executive VP of Member Services, Thrivent Financial for Lutherans.

I also want to express great appreciation to a group of colleagues who have been valued mentors and teachers: Roy Geer, Richard Leider, Larry Wilson, Fred Kiel, Rowland Moriarty, Daniel Goleman, Richard Boyatzis, Hersh Shefrin, Jeff Schwartz, Art Kleiner, and Arun Abey.

I would like to acknowledge my own financial adviser, Pete Silbaugh, CFP®. As my adviser for more than 20 years, Pete has demonstrated the integrity and client service orientation I so admire and need from my adviser. I am deeply grateful to my collaborating writer, Kathy Jordan, for helping give voice to my ideas and making the book-writing process productive and fun, and my agent, Esmond Harmsworth, for his insight.

Most of all, I would like to thank my wife Beth Ann, the most financially intelligent person I know, for her love and patience during the writing of this book.

Index